COOKING
with FIRE

French family recipes & more
for woodfire ovens

My thanks to my cousin, George Nercessian, who reintroduced me to the wonderful difference of cooking with woodfire. My gratitude to Alain Ephrem, the refractory manufacturer who helped make my start in this venture a lot easier than it might have been.

Thanks also to Karen Kaysing – she worked to shape my ideas and recipes into book form, which was no easy task. Without her patient help this process would have been much harder for me.

To my wife, Hilda, whose love and encouragement ("You can do anything, chéri.") sustained me through challenging times. To my sons: Jean-Paul, for his support at the factory and the office, and Alain, who gave me my two grandsons. And to all my family, friends and clients, who moved me to grow, experiment, improve and create better and better products.

I dedicate this book to my grandsons, Nicholas and Andrew, who have been my greatest inspiration. Since the age of three, Nicholas would always say, "Let's cook, Papa. I will help you." And Andrew, who watches as we work in the kitchen, and samples everything we make.

about
WOODFIRE OVENS

My recipes are very basic – like the oven. I don't like to complicate life, and I don't like to complicate my kitchen. A woodfire oven takes a long time to heat up by modern standards, but once it's hot there's a whole world of wonderfully simple food you can cook. With a little practice and planning, you will be able to create entire menus from a single fire.

For example, let's say you're planning to bake some pizzas. You'd build your fire according to instructions for pizza at a temperature of 600-700F, and then you're ready to bake. The leftover embers after making your pizzas are perfect for grilling your second course; then pop a tarte tatin or chocolate souffle into the oven afterward (with door closed) for a perfect end to a perfect meal.

Now let's take this one step farther and plan your whole weekend menu. The next morning (if you kept the door closed overnight), your oven will still be warm; you'll only need to fire it for 30-45 minutes to reach 550-600F, which is the perfect temperature for breakfast pizzas. Replace the door afterward; at lunchtime, the oven temperature will be ideal for roasting a chicken, along with an accompanying side of ratatouille or scalloped potatoes au gratin.

Once again keeping the door closed after cooking to retain heat, the oven will only need a short 30 minute firing in the evening for you to bake a macadamia crusted salmon and zucchini au gratin for dinner, followed by a rustic mixed berry croustade for dessert. What could be simpler or more ideal for entertaining? Once you get the hang of working with this oven, I know you'll love it as much as I do.

CONTENTS

COOKING with FIRE

STARTING the FIRE
We recommend using non-toxic fire starters, made of sawdust and paraffin. Put one square starter in the center of the oven floor. Place small pieces of wood* in criss-cross formation on top of the starter. Ignite starter.

When wood pieces begin to burn, add one piece of hardwood (2 to 2½" in diameter) to the pile. When the hardwood starts to burn, add another piece (do not add more than two pieces of hardwood at a time).

It is a good idea to keep a supply of small, 1" diameter pieces of wood on hand at all times, to jump start a fire or bring the oven quickly to a high temperature. If you use larger pieces of wood (2½" to 4" in diameter) heating time will be longer, but will accumulate more embers for roasting or barbecuing.

TYPES of WOOD
There are many varieties of wood which may be used to heat ovens. Each has an aroma of its own. Here is a partial list to stir your imagination:

Hardwoods (such as oak, maple, hickory, mesquite – all good for meat and barbecue)
Nut woods (such as almond, walnut, pecan – good for roasting)
Fruit woods [such as apple (good with pork), peach, apricot, plum, cherry (for barbecue)]
Olive (breads)
Citrus (lemon, grapefruit, orange – all good with fish)

Note: Pine, alder and other soft woods may be used to start the fire, but will not generate enough BTUs to get the oven to the necessary temperatures, nor will they leave embers to store heat on the oven floor.

For smoking meats, try alder chips, hickory, mesquite, cherry or Jack Daniels Barrel Chips. Soak for 15 minutes. Drain excess liquid and throw chips on embers. Close door. You may control the amount of smoke flavor by regulating how tightly the door is closed.

*Split a 14" piece of 2x4 into 3 sections, or use pieces of wood which are approximately 14" long and 1" thick. *• See DVD part 1/Section 2 for more on Oven Firing Basics*

COOKING TECHNIQUES

GRILLING   Firing time: 45 minutes - 1 hour, starting with a cold oven

Start a fire in the center of the oven floor. Keep fire burning for 45 minutes to 1 hour. There should be ample embers to grill meat, fish or vegetables. The longer the fire burns, the higher the temperature of the oven and the more ember accumulation there will be.

Spread embers on the floor of oven slightly larger than the size of the grill. Burning logs can be pushed to one side. Slide grill over embers and preheat for 5 minutes. Pull grill out and, using a clean rag or paper towel, lubricate grate with olive oil. Place items to be grilled on grate and slide back over embers. Any dripping will turn to ash because of the very high floor temperature. When grilling a thicker piece of meat or fish, move embers to either side of the grill, leaving 8" to 10 " of open space under the item to be grilled.

• See DVD 1/Section 4 for more on Grilling

BAKING PIZZA   Firing time: 1½ - 2 hours, starting with a cold oven

Start a fire in the center of the oven floor. After half an hour of firing, move the burning wood to the center left or center right. This is determined by which side of the oven will be used for baking the pizza (the heat has been stored in the floor beneath the fire; thus, when the pizza is placed on this spot, a better crust will be achieved).

Keep the fire burning until the temperature gauge registers at least 550F. Using the ash stick, move the embers to the side of the oven which will be most visible from the outside. You may start baking pizza when the temperature reaches 650 - 700F.

Using a brush, sweep ashes toward the fire. Wrap a damp towel around the brush, and mop the oven floor to remove any ash residue and cool the floor somewhat; this will help prevent crusts from being charred by the extreme initial temperature of the oven floor.

Place first pizza slightly closer to the oven opening (the tiles there are a little cooler by the door). After 30 seconds, move pizza further into oven, always checking the bottom of the crust. The second pizza can be placed deeper inside the oven. A constant flame 12 to 16" high should be maintained to ensure ample heat to bake the top of the pizza and maintain the temperature of the oven floor.   *• See DVD part 1/Section 3 for more on Baking Pizza*

COOKING TECHNIQUES continued

ROASTING   Firing time: 2 - 4 hours, starting with a cold oven (varies by volume of item to be roasted)

Chicken, turkey or prime rib: 2 hours

25 lb. suckling pig or game: 4 hours

Start a fire in the center of the oven and heat for desired time. After flames subside, move embers against the oven walls. Place item to be roasted in center of oven; close door. Starting temperature should be 500 - 525F. If oven is hotter, protect food with aluminum foil.

• *See DVD 1/Section 5 for more on Roasting a chicken*

BAKING BREADS, CAKES and PIES
Firing time: 2½ - 3 hours, starting with a cold oven

Start a fire in the center of the oven and keep fire going, maintaining temperature between 525 - 550F for bread baking, 475 - 500F for cakes and pies. Let fire burn out. Push embers to one side of oven. Using a long-handled peel or ashpan, shovel embers into 4 or 5 quart metal pot containing 2" of water. Carefully (pot will be very hot), cover pot with lid and remove to a non-combustible surface to cool. Brush remaining ashes to one corner of oven floor. Close oven door for 20 - 30 minutes to equalize oven temperature.

Remove door carefully – it will be very hot! Temperature should be about 500F. Mop floor of oven twice with damp towel. Put a small clean towel in metal pan containing ½" of water; place pan in corner of oven to provide moisture during first 10 minutes of baking.

Score the loaves and place on oven floor. Bread may be brushed with water, and the oven cavity sprayed with water, if desired. Close oven door tightly and do not open for first 10 minutes – you want to keep moisture inside. After 10 minutes, open oven to check that loaves are baking evenly. Remove pan with towel from oven. Replace oven door.

Depending on shape of loaves, it should take approximately 30 to 45 minutes for bread to bake. The internal temperature of the loaf should be 195 - 205F. Ten minutes before removing bread from oven, crack oven door to allow remaining steam to escape and give the bread a crisper crust. Allow bread to rest 20 - 60 minutes before serving.

Starting temperature should be 500F for bread baking, 450F for cakes and pies.

• *See DVD part 1/Section 6 and DVD part 2/Section 11 for more on Baking Bread*

THINGS to REMEMBER

The average log is 2½" by 14". Too many logs in the oven will choke the fire; never add more than 2 logs at a time.

Using small pieces of wood (i.e., 1 - 2" in diameter) will bring the oven to a higher temperature faster, but will not generate a lot of embers for roasting or barbecuing.

Combustion air (oxygen) is supplied from the lower area of the door opening; hot air and smoke is exhausted from the top of the door opening. For a smokier flavor, when pizza is done use a pizza peel to raise the pizza to 6" beneath the dome of the oven for 2 seconds.

The floor area nearest the door opening is always cooler than the rest of the oven floor. Items such as calzones or other dishes require less heat when the fire is on and the oven is at a higher temperature; for this reason they are generally placed near the door opening. When baking these dishes, it is necessary to rotate the food regularly to ensure they are baked evenly.

When barbecuing a thicker piece of meat, move the embers to either side of the grill, leaving a 10" area beneath the item being grilled free of direct heat. This indirect heat will slow the grilling and allow for even cooking.

When cooking other foods with an open flame ("pizza baking") or in a very hot oven, a double thickness of foil will help to bake without scorching.

When using ovenproof ceramic or glass dishes, remember to temper them before placing in the oven. This is achieved by placing the filled dish near the oven door opening for 10 seconds. Turn the plate, letting it warm another 10 seconds, then push the plate fully into the oven. Removing the hot dish from the oven to a cooler outside temperature means you must perform the tempering process in reverse: bring the hot dish near the door opening, wait 10 seconds, turn and wait another 10 seconds and then proceed.

The oven is designed to absorb and retain heat; the walls and dome are heat reservoirs. The longer the firing process, the longer the heat retention in the oven after the fire subsides, and the more cooking options you have for making multiple consecutive recipes as the oven slowly cools.

This is the only cooking appliance that uses three ways of introducing heat into the food:
1. Transmitting heat through direct contact;
2. Transmitting heat through convection (hot air circulated around product); and
3. Induction (radiating heat from mass surrounding the product).

A NOTE from MAURICE

I don't usually talk much about my own life, but I want to share with you my great passion for homestyle woodfire cooking - and to do that properly, I need to tell you who I am and how I got here.

I was born and raised on a farm on the outskirts of St. Loup, near Marseilles, France. Both my parents were Turkish-born Armenians, displaced by the Genocide and sent to live in France where they met and married. Although we lived only 30 minutes from the bustling port of Marseilles, in those pre-WWII days our tiny community in the middle of nowhere consisted of just a few families.

Those were hard times; by the end of WWII, my mother was widowed and left to care for three children by herself. Everything was scarce in those days - we had only what we could make or grow ourselves, and nothing was ever wasted. We grew fruits and vegetables, and raised rabbits, chickens, goats and sheep. We made our own cheese, olive oil, preserves and bread. We even made our own soap. Our house was large, but lacked running water or electricity; wood was our principal fuel, and it was used for all heating and cooking.

My mother was a wonderful cook - even though she often had little to work with. She was imaginative and creative, making do with whatever she could find in the garden or the cellar. She incorporated French flavors and cooking techniques into her traditional Armenian dishes with delicious results. Watching her prepare our meals, I developed a passion for food, and a deep respect for her approach to cooking. It made a profound impression that is with me to this day.

In 1956, at age 18, I came to the U.S. where I worked as an auto mechanic, eventually owning my own shop in Hollywood. My business grew, I got married and I settled into a comfortable life. Some years later on a trip home to Marseilles, my cousin invited us to visit his weekend farmhouse; I didn't know then that my life was about to change. The farmhouse had a handmade woodfire oven, and he offered to bake pizzas for us in that oven. I'll never forget that day – it was a rainy October afternoon, and the smoke from that fire blended deliciously, unforgettably, with the wet scent of autumn. As we sat on the covered patio, my cousin baked the pizzas while his wife poured wine, and we shared good conversation and good food, savoring the warmth of one another's company. Something really clicked for me that day – it was a sensory feast that stayed with me long after the day was done. I wanted to recreate the experience.

Back home in California, I looked for woodfire oven kits, but couldn't find any. Finally, I built my own oven, arranging fire bricks into a dome like the one I remembered from the village bakery of St. Loup; it wasn't pretty, but it worked.

I didn't know if these ovens would appeal to others as they had to me, but I wanted to find out. I sold my automotive business in 1986 and went to Marseilles to have some woodfire ovens made and shipped back to California. In 1987, I opened my first tiny showroom in Hollywood. I invited people from the press to come and taste my food. They came, they watched me cook in my woodfire oven, and they ate. And then they wrote. My business got more and more foot traffic as people came to see what all the buzz was about.

Over the next five years, I moved twice more to expand the business. In 2001, we moved to our current location in Glendale, where (in addition to our showroom and test kitchen) we manufacture and assemble ovens.

These beautiful ovens turn out some wonderful food, but in the end a woodfire oven is only as important as the people who appreciate and use it. This cookbook is my way of sharing my love for good food and warm companionship centered around the hearth – the woodfire experience that made such a powerful, lasting impact on me on that rainy October day long ago in Marseilles. I hope your woodfire cooking experiences bring you the same joy and satisfaction.

Bon appetit,

Maurice

BREADS

BAKING BREADS

There are few things more seductive or satisfying than the smell of bread baking, and fewer things harder to resist than the temptation of sampling a loaf fresh from the oven! The sight, the warmth and the aroma of freshly baked bread can make the 20-minute resting period seem like an eternity.

about LEAVENING AGENTS

There are many ways to bring bread dough alive, from adding leavening agents to waiting patiently for the yeast in the flour to develop in its moist environment (as in sourdough). Some of the most common leavening agents are:

FRESH COMPRESSED YEAST   Used mostly by commercial bakers. Lack of availability and short life (average shelf life is about two weeks) make it impractical for the home baker. Two-ounce blocks are sold in some markets.

ACTIVE DRY YEAST   The most convenient to use, active dry yeast is sold in packets and widely available in grocery stores. It is also available in professional supply stores in 16oz, vacuum-sealed packages. If stored in an airtight container and refrigerated, active dry yeast can last up to six months. This type of leavening agent must be activated in warm (105F) liquid before adding to flour.

INSTANT DRY YEAST   Sold in packets in most markets and professional supply stores. It may be mixed directly into flour and works very well in cold proofed doughs using cold (refrigerated) water. Customarily, proofing requires all liquids to be at 105F.

DOUBLE ACTING BAKING POWDER   Used to leaven cakes, cookies and some breads, it is called "double acting" because it will release carbon dioxide when in liquids and when heated.

BAKING SODA   Used to leaven cakes, cookies and some breads, baking soda will release carbon dioxide when in contact with acidic ingredients, such as milk, sour cream or fruit juice.

about SOURDOUGH

Small artisanal bakeries in France make sourdough bread, or pain au levain, only in wood-fired ovens. No commercial yeast is found in these bakeries. Most commercially produced sourdough breads are made with starters, but with the addition of commercial yeast to insure proper proofing.

Traditional sourdough bread is more nutritional, better for the digestive system and has a longer shelf life than mass produced, commercial varieties. It keeps well in the refrigerator for two to three weeks, and also freezes well. Slice bread before freezing and use as needed. Just toast slices and enjoy the great flavor!

There are a lot of ways to make a sourdough starter. Every baker has his or her own master starter – some are very old. They are freshened up daily or weekly. For the home baker, the starter can be dried and brought to life again with the addition of water. A starter can be made with just water and flour. Variations may also include the addition of figs, grapes, milk, or potato. The most important ingredients, however, are patience and ambient temperature.

If you follow some basic rules, it is very easy to make your own sourdough master starter. Use a good quality unbleached, all purpose flour (organic is preferred) and use bottled, non-carbonated water. It is important to proof your sourdough at room temperature (70 - 75F).

"LEVAIN" SOURDOUGH STARTER

In a quart glass jar, combine 1/2 cup unbleached all purpose flour with 1/2 cup bottled water (room temperature); mix well. Cover with plastic wrap and let stand at room temperature for three days, stirring once a day.

On the third day, add another 1/2 cup flour and 1/2 cup (less 1 tbsp) water to mixture, and stir well. Cover and allow to stand one more day at room temperature. After the next day, the mixture should be very bubbly and have a sour, but pleasant, aroma. *If is has an unpleasant aroma, discard and start again!*

Seal jar and store in refrigerator. Feed your starter 2 more days, then once a week, with 1/2 cup flour and 1/4 cup water. Mixture will be like thick cake batter or tomato paste. This is your master starter (or levain chef).

Remember to bring starter to room temperature for 3 hours before feeding, and allow to rest after feeding for 3 hours at room temperature before returning to refrigerator.

REFRESH SOURDOUGH STARTER
3⁄4 C starter
11⁄2 C bottled water (at room temp)
2 C unbleached all purpose flour

The day before making bread: At 3:00pm, remove jar of starter from refrigerator and allow to sit at room temperature (71 - 73F) for three hours. At 6:00pm, in a glass bowl or bowl of electric mixer, combine 3⁄4 cup starter, 11⁄2 cups water and 2 cups flour. Mix well. Cover with plastic wrap and let rest at room temperature overnight. The next day, remove 3⁄4 cup starter from bowl and save in refrigerator for next use.

DRY SOURDOUGH STARTER
If you aren't planning to make sourdough bread soon, you may wish to let your sourdough starter dry to preserve it. Spread your starter evenly in a thin flat layer on a Silpat baking mat. Air-dry for 3-4 days, or until thoroughly dry. Grind dried starter in a food processor, transfer to a glass jar. The dried powdered starter can be stored in the refrigerator for up to 6 months.

to REACTIVATE DRY SOURDOUGH STARTER: In a clean glass bowl, mix 1⁄2 C dry sourdough starter and 1⁄2 C room temperature bottled water. Cover with plastic wrap and let rest at room temperature for 24 hours. The next day the mixture should be bubbly and have a pleasant aroma. Add 1⁄2 C flour and 3 T room temperature bottled water; mix well and let stand for 8 hours covered with plastic wrap. Add another 1⁄2 C flour and 2 T water; mix again and leave at room temperature overnight. The following day your starter should be almost doubled in volume and ready to be used or refrigerated for use at a later date. The consistency should be that of tomato paste.

MIXING DOUGH by HAND
If you don't wish to use an electric mixer to make bread dough, follow these steps instead. Measure all but one cup of flour into large mixing bowl. Add the yeast and mix well with large wooden spoon. Form a well in center of flour. Add water mixture and olive oil. Using wooden spoon, mix together all ingredients, adding the remaining cup of flour, until dough is too stiff to continue. Knead dough by hand in bowl until all ingredients are incorporated. Turn dough onto lightly floured surface and knead until smooth, about 20 minutes. Shape into a ball, and place in an oiled bowl to proof, turning to coat all sides.

PAIN au LEVAIN
COUNTRY STYLE SOURDOUGH

This rustic sourdough has a thick, golden brown crust and supple crumb with large, irregular air pockets.

The day before baking, refresh sourdough starter as shown on page 18.

For bread dough:
2 T salt
2 C bottled water
8 C unbleached all purpose flour

Calculate temperature of water to be used for making dough. Using a base temperature of 215F, deduct the room temperature (RT) and the flour temperature (FT); what's left is the necessary temperature for the water. (For example: 215F minus RT 75F = 140, minus FT 74F = 66F correct water temperature.)

Attach paddle to electric mixer. Dissolve salt in water and add to mixing bowl with sourdough starter. Add 6 cups flour and mix on slow speed for 1 min. Replace paddle with dough hook. Increase to next speed and add remaining flour, 1/2 cup at a time. Dough will begin to pull away from sides of bowl. Add flour as needed until dough barely sticks to sides of bowl, about 10 to 12 min. total. Turn dough out onto lightly floured surface and knead until smooth and elastic, about 2 minutes. Rub a large bowl with olive oil and place dough in bowl, turning to coat with oil. Cover with plastic wrap and let proof at room temperature for an hour. Knead dough on floured surface for 30 seconds and return to bowl; cover with plastic wrap and let rest for another hour. Turn dough out and knead another 30 seconds. Divide dough into 3 equal portions and shape into loaves. Place loaves on well-floured wood peel or in canvas-covered baskets (panetons). Let proof for 3 hours covered with plastic wrap.

Meanwhile, start fire in the center of the oven. Keep it burning for 2 1/2 - 3 hours, maintaining a temperature of 525 - 550F. Let fire burn out. Push embers to one side. Using a long-handled peel or ashpan, shovel embers into large metal pot containing 2" of water. Carefully cover (very hot) pot with lid and remove to a fireproof surface to cool. Brush remaining ashes to one corner of oven floor. Close oven door for 20 - 30 min. Remove door carefully – it will be very hot! Temperature should be about 500F. Mop floor of oven twice with damp towel. Put a small clean towel and 1/2" of water in a metal pan; place pan in corner of oven to provide moisture during first 10 min. of baking.

Score loaves and place on oven floor. Bread may be brushed with water, and the oven cavity sprayed with water, if desired. Close oven door tightly and do not open for first 10 min., to keep moisture inside. After 10 min. open oven to check that loaves are baking evenly. Remove pan with towel from oven. Replace oven door.

Depending on shape of loaves, it should take approximately 30 - 45 min. for bread to bake. The internal temperature of the loaf should be 195 - 205F. Ten minutes before removing bread from oven, crack oven door to let steam escape and give the bread a crisper crust. Allow bread to rest 20 - 60 min. before serving.
• See DVD part 2/Section 11 for more on Bread

CORNBREAD

*Golden and flavorful with a very tender crumb, this bread
is best eaten still warm from the oven with a little butter
or creme fraiche and honey.*

1¼ C milk
1 large egg
1/3 C vegetable oil
1 C all-purpose flour (unbleached)
1 C yellow cornmeal
1½ tsp baking powder
½ tsp baking soda
¼ C sugar
1 tsp salt
¼ C corn kernels (optional)

Start fire in the center of the oven. Keep
it burning for 1½ - 2 hours, maintaining
a temperature of 525 - 550F. Let fire
burn out. Push embers to one side. Using a long-handled peel or ashpan, shovel
embers into large metal pot containing 2"
of water. Carefully cover (very hot) pot
with lid and remove to a fireproof surface
to cool. Brush remaining ashes to one
corner of oven floor. Close oven door for 20
- 30 min. Remove door carefully – it will
be very hot! Temperature should be about
500F.

In a large bowl, combine milk, egg and oil.
In a separate bowl, combine remaining dry
ingredients. Add dry mixture to milk mixture and stir just until blended; a few small
lumps may remain. Fold in optional corn
kernels, if desired.

Pour batter into a buttered cast iron skillet or cornbread pan. Bake in 500F oven
(no fire) until top is nicely browned and
toothpick inserted in center comes out clean
(approximately 15 minutes).
• See DVD part 1/Section 6 for more on Baking

PAIN BRIOCHE
FRENCH EGG BREAD
(from GILLES FOUCARD)

This bread makes a decadent and delicious French toast. My grandson, Nicholas, calls this treat 'SpongeBob Toast', since it's golden yellow with an airy texture, much like its namesake!

2 T salt
¾ C sugar
1¾ C bottled water at room temp.
8½ C unbleached all purpose flour
1 C butter, cut in ½-inch pieces, brought to room temp.
3 eggs
1 tsp instant yeast
2 C sourdough starter
1 T vegetable oil
2 T butter
1 egg
1 tsp water

Start fire in the center of the oven. Keep it burning for 2½ - 3 hours, maintaining a temperature of 525 - 550F. Let fire burn out. Push embers to one side. Using a long-handled peel or ashpan, shovel embers into large metal pot containing 2" of water. Carefully cover (very hot) pot with lid and remove to a fireproof surface to cool. Brush remaining ashes to one corner of oven floor. Close oven door for 20 - 30 min. Remove door carefully – it will be very hot! Let oven temperature cool to 450F.

Attach paddle to electric mixer. Dissolve salt and sugar in water, and add to mixing bowl. Add flour, butter pieces, eggs, yeast and sourdough starter, and mix at low speed for 3 minutes. Increase speed and continue mixing until smooth, about 2 minutes.

Turn dough out onto lightly floured work surface and knead for 15 seconds. Rub a large bowl with vegetable oil and place dough in bowl. Turn dough so that surface is coated with oil. Cover with plastic wrap and let dough rest at room temperature for 1 hour.

Knead dough again for about 15 seconds and return to same oiled bowl; cover with plastic wrap and let rest for another hour. Butter three 8½ x 4½ x 2½" loaf pans. Divide dough into three equal portions, and place in loaf pans. Let proof for about 3 hours.

Beat egg and water together, and brush tops of loaves. Bake at 450F (door closed, no embers) for approximately 30 minutes. (If top browns too fast, cover with a double layer of foil.) The internal temperature of the loaf should be 195F. Allow bread to rest 20 - 60 minutes before slicing.

• *See DVD part 1/Section 6 for more on Baking*

EGG BREAD

This versatile egg bread can also be adapted as a Challah recipe, by substituting water and olive oil for the dairy products. This tasty kosher variation appears at the end of the recipe.

7 C unbleached all-purpose flour
¼ C warm water (105-115F)
4 tsp active dry yeast
1 T salt
1 C sugar
1 C warm milk (105F)
4 eggs (room temperature)
½ C butter, melted and cooled to 105F
1 egg
1 T water
¼ C sesame seeds (optional)

Start fire in the center of the oven. Keep it burning for 2½ - 3 hours, maintaining a temperature of 525 - 550F. Let fire burn out. Push embers to one side. Using a long-handled peel or ashpan, shovel embers into large metal pot containing 2" of water. Carefully cover (very hot) pot with lid and remove to a fireproof surface to cool. Brush remaining ashes to one corner of oven floor. Close oven door for 20 - 30 min. Remove door carefully – it will be very hot! Let oven temperature cool to 450F.

In mixer fitted with paddle attachment, place 6 cups of flour. In separate bowl, combine water, yeast and 1 tablespoon of sugar; let stand for 10 minutes until creamy.

In another bowl, mix milk, salt and the remaining sugar. In yet another bowl, beat eggs well.

Turn mixer on low speed and add yeast mixture, milk mixture and eggs. Add melted butter and continue mixing for 1 minute. Replace paddle with dough hook. Mix for 1 minute at low speed, then increase to second speed, adding the remaining flour as needed until dough is smooth and elastic, about 4 minutes.

Turn dough out onto lightly floured surface. Knead for 30 seconds; shape into ball. Place dough into oiled bowl, turning to coat on all sides. Cover with plastic wrap and proof for 1½ hours (dough should double in size).

Turn dough onto lightly floured work surface. Fold dough over on itself 3 times and return to proofing bowl. Let rest for 1 more hour. Turn dough onto lightly floured work surface. Divide dough in half and divide each half into 3 equal portions. Roll out each portion into a thick rope about 13" long. Braid the dough into two loaves, tucking ends under. Place loaves on greased sheet pan and cover with plastic wrap. Let rise at room temperature for about 1 hour.

Beat egg with water. Brush tops of loaves with mixture and sprinkle with sesame seeds, if using.

Bake in 450F oven (door closed, no embers) for 30-35 minutes (to internal temperature of 195F). Note: If loaf tops brown too quickly, cover with double-folded foil.

For challah: Replace milk with 1 C water (105F) and substitute ½ C olive oil for the butter.

• See DVD part 1/Section 6 for more on Baking

TRADITIONAL BREAD

The ingredients are basic as can be, but this satisfying staple has nourished civilizations for centuries.

8 C unbleached all-purpose flour
4 tsp instant dry yeast
3 C cold bottled water
3 tsp salt

Measure 6 cups of flour into bowl of electric mixer with paddle attachment. Add yeast and mix for 3 seconds. In a quart measuring cup, add the water and salt; stir to dissolve.

Turn mixer on low and add water; mix for 2 minutes. Add 1 cup of flour, 1⁄2 cup at a time, mixing for one minute after each addition. Remove paddle and replace with dough hook. With mixer at low speed, add 1⁄2 cup of flour and mix for 1 minute; increase to second speed and add flour as needed until dough pulls away from sides of bowl, approximately 5 minutes.

Turn dough out onto lightly floured surface. Knead until smooth and elastic, about 2 minutes; shape into ball. Place dough into oiled bowl, turning to coat on all sides. Cover with plastic wrap and place in refrigerator overnight. (Proofing the dough for 24 hours will improve the flavor of the bread.)

Next day, start a fire in the center of the oven. Keep it burning for 2 - 21⁄2 hours, maintaining a temperature of 525 - 550F. Let fire burn out. Push embers to one side. Using a long-handled peel or ashpan, shovel embers into large metal pot containing 2" of water. Carefully cover (very hot) pot with lid and remove to a fireproof surface to cool. Brush remaining ashes to one corner of oven floor. Close oven door for 20 - 30 min. Remove door carefully – it will be very hot! Temperature should be about 500F. Mop floor of oven twice with damp towel. Put a small clean towel and 1⁄2" of water in a metal pan; place pan in corner of oven to provide moisture during first 10 min. of baking.

Turn dough onto work surface and knead, folding outer edges into center, for 2 minutes. Cover with towel and let rest for 30 minutes. Divide dough into four equal portions (about 16 oz. each). Form into desired shapes. Cover again and let dough rise for 11⁄2 hours on well-floured board or in bread baskets.

Score loaves and place on oven floor. Bread may be brushed with water, and the oven cavity sprayed with water, if desired. Close oven door tightly and do not open for first 10 min., to keep moisture inside. After 10 min. open oven to check that loaves are baking evenly. Remove pan with towel from oven. Replace oven door.

Depending on shape of loaves, it should take approximately 30 - 45 min. for bread to bake. The internal temperature of the loaf should be 195 - 205F. Ten minutes before removing bread from oven, crack oven door to let steam escape and give the bread a crisper crust. Allow bread to rest 20 - 60 min. before serving.

• *See DVD part 2/Section 11 for more on Bread*

MULTI-GRAIN BREAD

Healthy and hearty, this bread has a great texture and wonderfully earthy flavor.

7 C unbleached all-purpose flour
2 C multi-grain mix (oats, wheat and rye flakes, sesame and sunflower seeds, poppyseed, fine cracked wheat, *OR* pre-packaged multi-grain mix*)
4 tsp instant yeast
2 tsp salt
3 tsp sugar
¼ C olive oil
3 C bottled water (room temperature)
¼ C multi-grain mix (for coating outside of loaves)

*King Arthur sells a very good grain mix.

Start fire in the center of the oven. Keep it burning for 2½ - 3 hours, maintaining a temperature of 525 - 550F.
Let fire burn out. Push embers to one side. Using a long-handled peel or ashpan, shovel embers into large metal pot containing 2" of water. Carefully cover (very hot) pot with lid and remove to a fireproof surface to cool. Brush remaining ashes to one corner of oven floor. Close oven door for 20 - 30 min. Remove door carefully – it will be very hot! Temperature should be about 500F. Mop floor of oven twice with damp towel. Put a small clean towel and ½" of water in a metal pan; place pan in corner of oven to provide moisture during first 10 min. of baking.

In bowl of electric mixer fitted with paddle attachment, add 6 cups of flour, multi-grain mix and yeast; mix for 5 seconds. In a quart container, add the water, salt and sugar; stir to dissolve. Turn mixer on low and add water mixture and olive oil; mix for 2 minutes. Increase to second speed and add remaining 1 cup flour, ¼ cup at a time, until dough starts to pull away from sides of bowl and is a bit sticky, approximately 7 minutes.

Turn dough out onto lightly floured surface and knead until smooth and elastic, about 2 minutes. Place dough into bowl rubbed with olive oil, turning to coat on all sides. Cover with plastic wrap and allow dough to proof at room temperature for 1½ hours. Dough should almost double in size. Turn dough onto work surface and knead, folding outer edges into center 3 or 4 times. Divide dough into 3 equal portions. Form into desired shapes. Brush loaves with water and cover with multi-grain mixture. Place on wooden peels or well-floured counter top and cover with towel; let dough rise for 1½ hours.

Score loaves and place on oven floor. Spray the oven cavity with water, if desired. Close oven door tightly and do not open for first 10 min., to keep moisture inside. After 10 min. open oven to check that loaves are baking evenly. Remove pan with towel from oven. Replace oven door.

Depending on shape of loaves, it should take approximately 30 - 45 min. for bread to bake. The internal temperature of the loaf should be 195 - 205F. Ten minutes before removing bread from oven, crack oven door to let steam escape and give the bread a crisper crust. Allow bread to rest 20 - 60 min. before serving.

• *See DVD part 2/Section 11 for more on Bread*

RYE BREAD

This dense and hearty rye is rustic and flavorful. Try it with smoked salmon or shellfish, or just by itself with a little sweet butter.

Yeast Starter:
4 C unbleached all-purpose flour
1½ C bottled water (room temperature)
1 tsp salt
1 tsp sugar
2 tsp instant dry yeast

In bowl of electric mixer fitted with paddle attachment, mix flour and yeast for 3 seconds. In a quart container, add the water, salt and sugar; stir to dissolve. Turn on mixer and add water mixture; mix for 4 minutes. Remove paddle attachment, leaving yeast starter in bowl. Cover with plastic wrap and let proof at room temperature for 17 to 24 hours.

Rye Bread:
1½ C bottled water (room temperature)
2 tsp instant dry yeast
4 C rye flour
2 tsp salt

Start fire in the center of the oven. Keep it burning for 2 - 2½ hours, maintaining a temperature of 525 - 550F.
Let fire burn out. Push embers to one side. Using a long-handled peel or ashpan, shovel embers into large metal pot containing 2" of water. Carefully cover (very hot) pot with lid and remove to a fireproof surface to cool. Brush remaining ashes to one corner of oven floor. Close oven door for 20 - 30 min. Remove door carefully – it will be very hot! Temperature should be about 500F. Mop floor of oven twice with

damp towel. Put a small clean towel and ½" of water in a metal pan; place pan in corner of oven to provide moisture during first 10 min. of baking.

Attach dough hook to mixer. Mix dry yeast with 3 cups rye flour, and add to yeast starter in bowl of mixer; add water and mix at low speed. Add salt and mix for 3 minutes. Add remaining rye flour, ¼ cup at a time, until dough is elastic and not too sticky – about 3 more minutes. Turn dough out onto well floured surface and knead by hand about 2 minutes. Place dough into an oiled bowl, turning to coat on all sides. Cover with plastic wrap and let proof at room temp. for 1½ hours. (This dough will not expand as much as regular bread does.)

Turn dough onto well floured surface and knead, folding outer edges into center, for 1 minute. Divide into 3 equal portions; form into desired shapes. Place on wooden peels or well-floured counter top and cover with towel; let rise for 1 hour.

Score loaves and place on oven floor. Bread may be brushed with water, and the oven cavity sprayed with water, if desired. Close oven door tightly and do not open for first 10 min., to keep moisture inside. After 10 min. open oven to check that loaves are baking evenly. Remove pan with towel from oven. Replace oven door.

Depending on shape of loaves, it should take approximately 30 - 45 min. for bread to bake. The internal temperature of the loaf should be 195 - 205F. Ten minutes before removing bread from oven, crack oven door to let steam escape and give the bread a crisper crust. Allow bread to rest 20 - 60 min. before serving.
• *See DVD part 2/Section 11 for more on Bread*

27

BUTTERNUT SQUASH BREAD

This sweet, moist treat is reminiscent of zucchini bread.
Warning: people always ask for seconds and it disappears
very quickly!

butter
flour
2 C unbleached all-purpose flour
2 tsp baking powder
1⁄2 tsp baking soda
1⁄4 tsp salt
1 tsp ground cinnamon
1⁄4 tsp ground nutmeg
3 eggs (room temperature)
1 C sugar
1 C vegetable oil
2 tsp vanilla extract
4 C shredded (raw) butternut squash
1 C chopped walnuts
1 C chocolate chips*
*Note: For a healthier alternative, substitute chopped
dates in place of chocolate chips.*

Start fire in the center of the oven. Keep
it burning for 2 - 2 1⁄2 hours, maintaining a temperature of 525 - 550F. Let
fire burn out. Push embers to one side.
Using a long-handled peel or ashpan,
shovel embers into large metal pot
containing 2" of water. Carefully cover
(very hot) pot with lid and remove to a
fireproof surface to cool. Brush remaining ashes to one corner of oven floor.
Close oven door for 20 - 30 min. Remove door carefully – it will be very hot!
Temperature should be about 500F.

Butter and flour two 8 x 4 x 2 1⁄4" loaf pans.
Sift together flour, baking powder and soda,
salt, cinnamon and nutmeg.

In a mixer fitted with whip attachment, beat
eggs for 2 minutes. Add sugar 1 tablespoon
at a time, mixing 30 seconds after each addition.

With mixer on, slowly add oil. Mix for 2
minutes more. Add vanilla and flour mixture. Mix for 10 seconds until well blended.
With a large rubber spatula, fold in the
squash, nuts and chocolate chips until well
incorporated.

 Divide batter evenly between loaf pans and
bake in 400-500F oven (door closed, no
embers) for 45 minutes.

Bread will keep for 3 days at room temperature; 2 weeks if refrigerated; one month in
the freezer, or 6 months if vacuum-packed.
• See DVD part 1/Section 6 for more on Baking

PIZZA

ITALIAN PIZZA DOUGH

The first pizza I ever had was baked in a sheet tray and had only tomato sauce, anchovies and black olives. Street vendors sold it by the square, and it was a treat!

Traditional Italian pizzas have very few toppings, typically just fresh tomato sauce or chopped tomatoes and a little mozzarella cheese. The crust is very thin and flaky.

3 C cake flour (or 4 C imported Capputo flour; if using, omit the all purpose flour)
2 tsp instant yeast
1½ tsp salt
1¾ C refrigerated water
1 C all purpose flour

In bowl of electric mixer fixed with paddle attachment, combine cake flour and yeast. Add salt to water; mix well. With mixer on low speed, add water all at once and mix for 2 minutes. Replace paddle with dough hook attachment and mix at low speed for 1 minute. Increase to second speed and gradually add all-purpose flour. Continue mixing until dough pulls away from sides of the bowl, approximately 5 minutes.

Turn out dough onto floured surface. Knead by hand for 2 minutes until smooth and elastic.

Divide into 4 (8 oz.) portions (or 5 6-oz. portions for very thin crust pizza shells). Coat each doughball with flour or olive oil and place in plastic bags or plastic container. Refrigerate 18 to 24 hours before using. Refrigerate or freeze dough which will not be used within 3 days.

When ready to use, remove doughballs from refrigerator and bring to room temperature for 15 to 20 minutes. Work each ball to a flat 11-inch circle. Let pizza shell rest 20 minutes on counter top before adding toppings.

to PREPARE by HAND

In a large bowl or on countertop, combine cake flour and yeast. Make well in center. Mix salt with water; pour in flour well. Using fingers or a wooden spoon, mix flour and water, working from the center out, until all flour has been incorporated Add all purpose flour and knead dough until smooth and elastic, 15 to 20 min.

• See DVD part 1/Section 7 for more on Pizza Dough

MAURICE'S PIZZA DOUGH

Every pizza chef is proud of his or her own dough, and I'm no exception. Try this one and see what you think.

1 tsp sugar
3 tsp salt
3 C refrigerator-cold, bottled water
1 C semolina
7 C all-purpose flour (unbleached)
4 tsp instant yeast
2 T dried thyme (optional)
¼ C olive oil

Dissolve sugar and salt in cold water.

Install paddle attachment to electric mixer. Put the semolina and 5 cups of the flour in bowl of mixer; add yeast and mix at low speed until well blended. Add water mixture and oil, and mix at the next speed for approximately 2 minutes.

Install hook attachment. Continue mixing at the same speed while adding remaining flour, ½ cup at a time, until dough clings to hook. Mix 5 minutes more, until dough is smooth and no longer sticks to sides of bowl. (Flour may be added as needed.)

Remove dough from bowl and knead by hand for 2 minutes.

Punch down dough and divide into 8 portions (each portion will be about 8 oz and will make an 11" pizza). Coat each doughball with flour or olive oil and place in plastic bags or plastic container. Refrigerate 18 to 24 hours before using. (It will keep up to two more days in refrigerator, or up to one month in freezer.)

When ready to use, remove doughballs from refrigerator and bring to room temperature for 15 - 20 minutes. Work each ball to a flat 11" circle. Let pizza shell rest 20 minutes on counter top before adding toppings.

• See DVD part 1/Section 7 for more on Pizza Dough

HOMEMADE PIZZA SAUCE

*If you grow your own tomatoes, take advantage of the
bounty to make extra sauce and freeze it.*

2 T olive oil
1 medium yellow onion, diced
2 garlic cloves, chopped
2 lbs. ripe Roma tomatoes, peeled, seeded
and chopped
1 T herbes de Provence
salt and pepper to taste
2 T chopped fresh basil

In saucepan, heat oil. Saute onion until translucent. Add garlic and cook 1 minute longer. Stir
in tomatoes and herbs, and continue to simmer
15 to 20 minutes longer, until sauce thickens.

Adjust seasoning as necessary to taste. Add
basil. Yields approximately 2 cups.

*Sauce may be used immediately, or may be refrigerated for up to
one week. The sauce will also freeze nicely for 3 months.*

QUICK PIZZA SAUCE

*Sometimes you just want a great pizza without a lot of
bother.*

1 - 15 oz. can tomato sauce
1 - 15 oz. can crushed tomatoes, drained
2 T herbes de Provence

Combine all ingredients together and blend
well. Yields approximately 4½ cups.

*Sauce may be used immediately, or may be refrigerated
for up to one week. The sauce will also freeze nicely for 3
months.*

THIN CRUST APPETIZER PIZZA

You'll be surprised at how so little topping can deliver such big taste!

Makes one pizza

11" pizza shell
(made from 6oz Italian-style dough)
olive oil
3 cloves garlic, chopped
1 T each fresh basil, oregano, thyme – finely chopped
¼ C shredded mozzarella cheese
¼ C grated parmesan cheese
½ C chopped tomatoes

Start a fire in the center of the oven floor. After half an hour of firing, move the burning wood to the center left or center right. This is determined by which side of the oven will be used for baking the pizza (the heat has been stored in the floor beneath the fire; thus, when the pizza is placed on this spot, a better crust will be achieved).

Keep the fire burning until the temperature gauge registers at least 550F. Using the ash stick, move the embers to the side of the oven which will be most visible from the outside. You may start baking pizza when the temperature reaches 650 - 700F.

Using a brush, sweep ashes toward the fire. Wrap a damp towel around the brush, and mop the oven floor to remove any ash residue and cool the floor somewhat; this will help prevent crusts from being charred by the extreme initial temperature of the oven floor.

Place pizza slightly closer to the oven opening (the tiles there are a little cooler by the door). After 30 seconds, move pizza further into oven, always checking the bottom of the crust. The next pizza (if you're making more than one) can be placed deeper inside the oven. A constant flame 12 to 16" high should be maintained to ensure ample heat to bake the top of the pizza and maintain the temperature of the oven floor.

Brush shell with olive oil. Sprinkle with ingredients in order given.

Bake for 3 minutes, or until done, in 600 - 700F oven (fire on, door off). Slice and serve.
• See DVD part 2/Section 2 for more on Thin Crust Pizza

BBQ CHICKEN PIZZA

A true American classic, and with very good reason!

Makes one pizza

11" pizza (made from 8 oz. pizza dough)
olive oil
½ C pizza tomato sauce
1 C shredded jalapeno jack cheese
1 C chopped, steamed chicken breast (see below) or other precooked chicken breast
½ C your favorite spicy bbq sauce
12 thin-sliced red onion rings
¼ C chopped cilantro

To steam chicken: (if using precooked chicken, omit this step)
1 C white wine or water
1 boneless chicken breast
½ tsp salt
½ tsp ground pepper
½ tsp dried thyme

In 2-quart pot fitted with steamer rack, bring liquid to boil. Season chicken breast with salt, pepper and thyme. Place chicken on steaming rack and lower heat. Cover pot and steam for about 7 minutes (internal temperature should be about 120F - chicken will continue to cook on pizza). Allow chicken to cool and chop into ½" pieces.

Start a fire in the center of the oven floor. After half an hour of firing, move the burning wood to the center left or center right. This is determined by which side of the oven will be used for baking the pizza (the heat has been stored in the floor beneath the fire; thus, when the pizza is placed on this spot, a better crust will be achieved). Keep the fire burning until the temperature gauge registers at least 550F. Using the ash stick, move the embers to the side of the oven which will be most visible from the outside. You may start baking pizza when the temperature reaches 650 - 700F.

Using a brush, sweep ashes toward the fire. Wrap a damp towel around the brush, and mop the oven floor to remove any ash residue and cool the floor somewhat; this will help prevent crusts from being charred by the extreme initial temperature of the oven floor.

Place pizza slightly closer to the oven opening (the tiles there are a little cooler by the door). After 30 seconds, move pizza further into oven, always checking the bottom of the crust. The next pizza (if you're making more than one) can be placed deeper inside the oven. A constant flame 12 - 16" high should be maintained to ensure ample heat to bake the top of the pizza and maintain the temperature of the oven floor.

Brush pizza dough with olive oil. Spread shell with tomato sauce, leaving a ¾" border. Top with half the cheese. Toss chicken with bbq sauce and arrange over cheese. Top with remaining cheese and onion rings.

Bake in 600 - 700F oven (door off, fire on one side) for 3 to 4 minutes. Place on serving platter and let rest for 2 minutes. Sprinkle with cilantro, slice and serve.

• See DVD part 1/Section 3 for more on Pizza

STEAK PIZZA

What could be better than steak and pizza combined into one dish?

Makes one pizza

11" pizza (made from 8 oz. pizza dough)
1 T olive oil
1 T butter
1 - 8oz. ribeye or top sirloin steak
salt and pepper to taste
1 bell pepper, thinly sliced
1 medium yellow onion, thinly sliced
olive oil
¼ C pizza sauce
1 C shredded jalapeno jack cheese

Start a fire in the center of the oven floor. After half an hour of firing, move the burning wood to the center left or center right. This is determined by which side of the oven will be used for baking the pizza (the heat has been stored in the floor beneath the fire; thus, when the pizza is placed on this spot, a better crust will be achieved). Keep the fire burning until the temperature gauge registers at least 550F. Using the ash stick, move the embers to the side of the oven which will be most visible from the outside. You may start baking pizza when the temperature reaches 650 - 700F.

Using a brush, sweep ashes toward the fire. Wrap a damp towel around the brush, and mop the oven floor to remove any ash residue and cool the floor somewhat; this will help prevent crusts from being charred by the extreme initial temperature of the oven floor.

Place pizza slightly closer to the oven opening (the tiles there are a little cooler by the door). After 30 seconds, move pizza further into oven, always checking the bottom of the crust. The next pizza (if you're making more than one) can be placed deeper inside the oven. A constant flame 12 - 16" high should be maintained to ensure ample heat to bake the top of the pizza and maintain the temperature of the oven floor.

In large skillet, heat oil and butter. Season steak with salt and pepper, and cook in pan for about 4 minutes on each side (internal temperature should be 125F – meat will cook further on pizza).

Using the same skillet, saute bell pepper until soft; remove from pan and set aside. Adding more oil if necessary, cook onion on low heat until translucent. Set aside. Cut steak across grain into thin slices.

Brush pizza shell with olive oil. Spread tomato sauce on pizza shell, leaving a ¾" border. Sprinkle with half the cheese, and top with meat, peppers and onion. Cover with remaining cheese.

Bake in 600 - 700F oven (door off, fire on one side) for 3 - 4 minutes. Place on serving platter and let rest for 3 minutes before slicing.
• *See DVD part 1/Section 3 for more on Pizza*

SHRIMP PIZZA

This is another example of a simple pizza with few ingredients that packs an enormous amount of flavor.

Makes one pizza

11" pizza (made from 8 oz. pizza dough)
1⁄4 C your favorite prepared pesto
11⁄2 C shredded mozzarella
10 medium raw shrimp, shelled and deveined
12 thinly sliced red onion rings

Start a fire in the center of the oven floor. After half an hour of firing, move the burning wood to the center left or center right. This is determined by which side of the oven will be used for baking the pizza (the heat has been stored in the floor beneath the fire; thus, when the pizza is placed on this spot, a better crust will be achieved). Keep the fire burning until the temperature gauge registers at least 550F. Using the ash stick, move the embers to the side of the oven which will be most visible from the outside. You may start baking pizza when the temperature reaches 600F.

Using a brush, sweep ashes toward the fire. Wrap a damp towel around the brush, and mop the oven floor to remove any ash residue and cool the floor somewhat; this will help prevent crusts from being charred by the extreme initial temperature of the oven floor.

Place pizza slightly closer to the oven opening (the tiles there are a little cooler by the door). After 30 seconds, move pizza further into oven, always checking the bottom of the crust. The next pizza (if you're making more than one) can be placed deeper inside the oven. A constant flame 12 - 16" high should be maintained to ensure ample heat to bake the top of the pizza and maintain the temperature of the oven floor.

Spread pesto on pizza shell. Top with half the mozzarella cheese. Slice shrimp in half lengthwise and arrange on pizza. Top with remaining cheese and onion rings.

Bake in 600F oven (door off, fire on one side) for 3 - 4 minutes. Place on serving platter and let rest for 3 minutes before slicing.

• See DVD part 1/Section 3 for more on Pizza

SEAFOOD PIZZA

A casually elegant pizza, this unbeatable recipe comes from my friend Ed La Dou.
It's simple to prepare, and guaranteed to make any occasion more special.

Makes one pizza

BASE SAUCE
3 T sour cream
1 tsp lemon or lime juice
1 tsp chopped fresh fennel or dill
1 T golden caviar
salt and white pepper to taste

olive oil
11" pizza (made from 8 oz. pizza dough)
8 medium fresh shrimp, shelled, cleaned
and butterflied
½ C scallops, chopped
½ C mozzarella cheese, shredded
red onion, sliced thinly in rings
chives, chopped

Start a fire in the center of the oven floor. After half an hour of firing, move the burning wood to the center left or center right. This is determined by which side of the oven will be used for baking the pizza (the heat has been stored in the floor beneath the fire; thus, when the pizza is placed on this spot, a better crust will be achieved). Keep the fire burning until the temperature gauge registers at least 550F. Using the ash stick, move the embers to the side of the oven which will be most visible from the outside. You may start baking pizza when the temperature reaches 600F.

Using a brush, sweep ashes toward the fire. Wrap a damp towel around the brush, and mop the oven floor to remove any ash residue and cool the floor somewhat; this will help prevent crusts from being charred by the extreme initial temperature of the oven floor.

Place pizza slightly closer to the oven opening (the tiles there are a little cooler by the door). After 30 seconds, move pizza further into oven, always checking the bottom of the crust. The next pizza (if you're making more than one) can be placed deeper inside the oven. A constant flame 12 - 16" high should be maintained to ensure ample heat to bake the top of the pizza and maintain the temperature of the oven floor.

Combine sauce ingredients. Set aside.

Brush pizza shell with olive oil (this seals it from absorbing liquid). Spread sauce on pizza shell. Arrange shrimp and scallops, and top with cheese. Place individual onion rings over cheese.

Bake in 600F oven (door off, fire on one side) for 3 - 4 minutes. Sprinkle with chopped chives. Place on serving platter and let rest for 3 minutes before slicing.
• See DVD part 1/Section 3 for more on Pizza

ESCARGOT PIZZA

I have a friend who will not eat anything exotic or unusual. I told him this was a spicy mushroom pizza... After he ate a slice and loved it, I confessed that it was really escargots (snails) – and he ate two more slices!

Makes one pizza

11" pizza (made from 8 oz. pizza dough)
1 T olive oil
3 cloves garlic, finely chopped
3 large ripe tomatoes, peeled, seeded and chopped
1 T wine vinegar
2 T butter
1 tsp dried thyme
2 T chopped parsley
salt and pepper to taste
6 oz. can prepared escargots,* rinsed and cut in half
1 C shredded gruyere *or* mozzarella cheese
Escargots can be found in the gourmet section of most major supermarkets.

Start a fire in the center of the oven floor. After half an hour of firing, move the burning wood to the center left or center right. This is determined by which side of the oven will be used for baking the pizza (the heat has been stored in the floor beneath the fire; thus, when the pizza is placed on this spot, a better crust will be achieved). Keep the fire burning until the temperature gauge registers at least 550F. Using the ash stick, move the embers to the side of the oven which will be most visible from the outside. You may start baking pizza when the temperature reaches 600-700F.
Using a brush, sweep ashes toward the fire. Wrap a damp towel around the brush, and mop the oven floor to remove any ash residue and cool the floor somewhat; this will help prevent crusts from being charred by the extreme initial temperature of the oven floor.

Place pizza slightly closer to the oven opening (the tiles there are a little cooler by the door). After 30 seconds, move pizza further into oven, always checking the bottom of the crust. The next pizza (if you're making more than one) can be placed deeper inside the oven. A constant flame 12 - 16" high should be maintained to ensure ample heat to bake the top of the pizza and maintain the temperature of the oven floor.

In skillet, heat olive oil. Add garlic and cook over low heat for about 30 seconds; do not brown. Add chopped tomatoes and vinegar, and cook until liquid has evaporated. Remove from heat and add butter, thyme, parsley, salt and pepper. Stir until butter is melted.

Spread 1/2 cup of the tomato-herb mixture on pizza shell leaving a 1/2" border. Top with half of cheese. Evenly arrange escargot over shell, and top with remaining cheese.

Bake in 600-700F oven (door off, fire on one side) for 3 - 4 minutes. Place on serving platter and let rest for 3 minutes before slicing.

• *See DVD part 1/Section 3 for more on Pizza*

FIG and PROSCIUTTO PIZZA

A truly awesome pizza, this variation of my friend Evelyn Slomon's gourmet fig pizza is a little sweet, a little salty and thoroughly delicious. Try it, you won't be sorry!

Makes one pizza

11" pizza (made from 8 oz. pizza dough)
olive oil
¼ C tomato pizza sauce
1 C shredded mozzarella cheese
4 large fresh figs, each cut into 8 pieces*
2½ oz. fresh goat cheese
5 slices prosciutto
8 leaves arugula
If fresh figs are not available, substitute sliced dates.

Start a fire in the center of the oven floor. After half an hour of firing, move the burning wood to the center left or center right. This is determined by which side of the oven will be used for baking the pizza (the heat has been stored in the floor beneath the fire; thus, when the pizza is placed on this spot, a better crust will be achieved). Keep the fire burning until the temperature gauge registers at least 550F. Using the ash stick, move the embers to the side of the oven which will be most visible from the outside. You may start baking pizza when the temperature reaches 600-700F.
Using a brush, sweep ashes toward the fire. Wrap a damp towel around the brush, and mop the oven floor to remove any ash residue and cool the floor some-

what; this will help prevent crusts from being charred by the extreme initial temperature of the oven floor.

Place pizza slightly closer to the oven opening (the tiles there are a little cooler by the door). After 30 seconds, move pizza further into oven, always checking the bottom of the crust. The next pizza (if you're making more than one) can be placed deeper inside the oven. A constant flame 12 - 16" high should be maintained to ensure ample heat to bake the top of the pizza and maintain the temperature of the oven floor.

Brush pizza dough with olive oil. Spread shell with pizza sauce, leaving a ¾" border. Top with half the mozzarella. Arrange figs over cheese, and top with remaining mozzarella. Dot with goat cheese.

Bake in 600-700F oven (door off, fire on one side) for 3 - 4 minutes. Place on serving platter and let rest for 3 minutes. Arrange prosciutto slices over pizza and cut into 8 pieces. Top each piece with arugula and serve.
• See DVD part 1/Section 9 for more on Fig and Prosciutto Pizza

LAHMAJOON
SPICY MIDDLE EASTERN PIZZA

Don't be afraid to use a liberal hand with the garlic and hot sauce – the more you use, the more your guests will enjoy this bold and spicy pizza

Makes 2 pizzas

2 10" pizzas (each made from 6 oz. pizza dough)
10 oz. ground beef or lamb
¼ C onion, chopped fine
¼ C scallions, chopped fine
2 ripe tomatoes, chopped (or a 14 oz. can chopped tomatoes, drained)
2 T chopped garlic (or more to taste)
2 T chopped parsley
¼ C chopped bell peppers
2 T tomato paste
1 tsp kosher salt
1 tsp freshly ground black pepper
½ tsp ground cumin
hot sauce to taste
olive oil for brushing

Start a fire in the center of the oven floor. After half an hour of firing, move the burning wood to the center left or center right. This is determined by which side of the oven will be used for baking the pizza (the heat has been stored in the floor beneath the fire; thus, when the pizza is placed on this spot, a better crust will be achieved). Keep the fire burning until the temperature gauge registers at least 550F. Using the ash stick, move the embers to the side of the oven which will be most visible from the outside. You may start baking pizza when the temperature reaches 600-700F.

Using a brush, sweep ashes toward the fire. Wrap a damp towel around the brush, and mop the oven floor to remove any ash residue and cool the floor somewhat; this will help prevent crusts from being charred by the extreme initial temperature of the oven floor.

Place pizza slightly closer to the oven opening (the tiles there are a little cooler by the door). After 30 seconds, move pizza further into oven, always checking the bottom of the crust. The next pizza (if you're making more than one) can be placed deeper inside the oven. A constant flame 12 - 16" high should be maintained to ensure ample heat to bake the top of the pizza and maintain the temperature of the oven floor.

In mixing bowl, combine well all ingredients except olive oil. Marinate in refrigerator for at least 2 hours.

Brush shells with olive oil. Divide meat mixture evenly into 2 portions (about 1 cup for each pizza) and spread on shells, allowing ½ inch border.

Bake in 600-700F oven (door off, fire on one side) for 3 - 4 minutes. Cut into portions and serve with lemon wedges.

NOTE: For a richer pizza, sprinkle with ½ C shredded mozzarella cheese before baking. For more of a "kick," sprinkle with chopped jalapeno.
• See DVD part 1/Section 3 for more on Pizza

MEDITERRANEAN PIZZA

Bursting with the flavors of that sunny region

Makes one pizza

11" pizza (made from 8 oz. pizza dough)
olive oil
1 T chopped garlic
1/4 C sliced black imported olives
1/4 C crumbled feta cheese
1/4 C shredded mozzarella
1/2 C chopped tomatoes
2 T chopped fresh oregano, basil or thyme, or combination of all three
1/4 C chopped red onion (optional)

Start a fire in the center of the oven floor. After half an hour of firing, move the burning wood to the center left or center right. This is determined by which side of the oven will be used for baking the pizza (the heat has been stored in the floor beneath the fire; thus, when the pizza is placed on this spot, a better crust will be achieved). Keep the fire burning until the temperature gauge registers at least 550F. Using the ash stick, move the embers to the side of the oven which will be most visible from the outside. You may start baking pizza when the temperature reaches 600-700F.

Using a brush, sweep ashes toward the fire. Wrap a damp towel around the brush, and mop the oven floor to remove any ash residue and cool the floor somewhat; this will help prevent crusts from being charred by the extreme initial temperature of the oven floor.

Place pizza slightly closer to the oven opening (the tiles there are a little cooler by the door). After 30 seconds, move pizza further into oven, always checking the bottom of the crust. The next pizza (if you're making more than one) can be placed deeper inside the oven. A constant flame 12 - 16" high should be maintained to ensure ample heat to bake the top of the pizza and maintain the temperature of the oven floor.

Brush pizza shell with olive oil. Sprinkle shell with garlic, leaving a 1/2" border. Top with olives, cheeses, tomatoes and herbs. Sprinkle with onions, if using.

Bake in 600-700F oven (door off, fire on one side) for 3 - 4 minutes. Place on serving platter and let rest for 2-3 minutes before slicing.

• See DVD part 1/Section 3 for more on Pizza

CARAMELIZED ONION PIZZA

A particularly good example of a "white" pizza (no tomato, no meat)
- just a few simple ingredients, but everybody loves this one!

Makes one pizza

11" pizza (made from 8 oz. pizza dough)
olive oil
1 C shredded mozzarella cheese
½ C caramelized onions (see below)
½ C feta cheese
2 T pine nuts

To caramelize onions: (makes enough for two pizzas)
½ C olive oil
3 C sliced onions
½ tsp sugar (omit if sweet onions are used)

Dissolve sugar in oil in 12" skillet. Heat oil and add onions. Cook on very low heat until onions are soft and translucent. Drain off all excess oil. (Onions may be refrigerated for 3 - 4 days, or frozen up to 2 months. I recommend making 3 to 4 portions at a time.)

Start a fire in the center of the oven floor. After half an hour of firing, move the burning wood to the center left or center right. This is determined by which side of the oven will be used for baking the pizza (the heat has been stored in the floor beneath the fire; thus, when the pizza is placed on this spot, a better crust will be achieved). Keep the fire burning until the temperature gauge registers at least 550F. Using the ash stick, move the embers to the side of the oven which will be most visible from the outside. You may start baking pizza when the temperature reaches 600-700F. Using a brush, sweep ashes toward the fire. Wrap a damp towel around the brush, and mop the oven floor to remove any ash residue and cool the floor somewhat; this will help prevent crusts from being charred by the extreme initial temperature of the oven floor.

Place pizza slightly closer to the oven opening (the tiles there are a little cooler by the door). After 30 seconds, move pizza further into oven, always checking the bottom of the crust. The next pizza (if you're making more than one) can be placed deeper inside the oven. A constant flame 12 - 16" high should be maintained to ensure ample heat to bake the top of the pizza and maintain the temperature of the oven floor.

Brush pizza dough with olive oil. Top with half the mozzarella. Spread caramelized onions over top and cover with remaining mozzarella and feta cheese. Sprinkle with pine nuts.

Bake in 600-700F oven (door off, fire on one side) for 3 - 4 minutes. Place on serving platter and let rest for 2-3 minutes before slicing.
• *See DVD part 1/Section 8 for more on Caramelized Onion Pizza*

FLAMMEKUCHE
ALSATIAN PIZZA
You have to taste this rich, thin-crust pizza to believe it - luxurious!

Makes one pizza

11-12" pizza (made from 7oz. pizza dough)

SAUCE
¼ C cream cheese + ¼ C sour cream
or substitute ½ C creme fraiche
salt and pepper to taste

TOPPING
1 C diced onions
¼ C olive oil
½ C French style ham, sliced in 1/2" strips
1 C shredded gruyere or emmenthaler cheese

Start a fire in the center of the oven floor. After half an hour of firing, move the burning wood to the center left or center right. This is determined by which side of the oven will be used for baking the pizza (the heat has been stored in the floor beneath the fire; thus, when the pizza is placed on this spot, a better crust will be achieved). Keep the fire burning until the temperature gauge registers at least 550F. Using the ash stick, move the embers to the side of the oven which will be most visible from the outside. You may start baking pizza when the temperature reaches 600-700F.
Using a brush, sweep ashes toward the fire. Wrap a damp towel around the brush, and mop the oven floor to remove any ash residue and cool the floor somewhat; this will help prevent crusts from being charred by the extreme initial temperature of the oven floor.

Place pizza slightly closer to the oven opening (the tiles there are a little cooler by the door). After 30 seconds, move pizza further into oven, always checking the bottom of the crust. The next pizza (if you're making more than one) can be placed deeper inside the oven. A constant flame 12 - 16" high should be maintained to ensure ample heat to bake the top of the pizza and maintain the temperature of the oven floor.

Cook diced onions in olive oil very slowly until translucent. This will result in ½ cup cooked onions.

Combine cream mixture with salt and pepper. Spread on pizza shell and top with half the cheese. Arrange the onions and ham, and cover with the remaining cheese.

Bake in 600-700F oven (door off, fire on one side) for 3 - 4 minutes. Place on serving platter and let rest for 3 minutes before slicing.
• *See DVD part 1/Section 3 for more on Pizza*

ROASTED VEGGIE PIZZA with YOGURT SAUCE

In the unlikely event you have any pizza left over, this is excellent eaten cold the next day!

Makes one pizza

11" pizza (made from 8 oz. pizza dough
1 Japanese eggplant
1 zucchini
1 bell pepper
½ C olive oil

NOTE: These vegetables make enough topping for two pizzas – refrigerate or freeze leftover roasted veggies for later use.

olive oil
¼ C tomato pizza sauce
1 C shredded smoked Gouda cheese

YOGURT SAUCE
½ C plain yogurt
1 large clove garlic, pressed
salt to taste

Start a fire in the center of the oven floor. After half an hour of firing, move the burning wood to the center left or center right. This is determined by which side of the oven will be used for baking the pizza (the heat has been stored in the floor beneath the fire; thus, when the pizza is placed on this spot, a better crust will be achieved). Keep the fire burning until the temperature gauge registers at least 550F. Using the ash stick, move the embers to the side of the oven which will be most visible from the outside. You may start baking pizza when the temperature reaches 600-700F. Using a brush, sweep ashes toward the fire. Wrap a damp towel around the brush, and mop the oven floor to remove any ash residue and cool the floor some-what; this will help prevent crusts from being charred by the extreme initial temperature of the oven floor.

Place pizza slightly closer to the oven opening (the tiles there are a little cooler by the door). After 30 seconds, move pizza further into oven, always checking the bottom of the crust. The next pizza (if you're making more than one) can be placed deeper inside the oven. A constant flame 12 - 16" high should be maintained to ensure ample heat to bake the top of the pizza and maintain the temperature of the oven floor.

Slice zucchini and eggplant lengthwise in ¼" slices. Brush both sides with olive oil and place on baking sheet, together with whole bell pepper. Roast in oven with open flame for 5 to 10 minutes, or until eggplant and zucchini are nicely browned and bell pepper is blackened all over.

Cut zucchini and eggplant into ½" strips. Peel and cut bell pepper into ½" strips (you should have about 12 strips of each vegetable).

Brush pizza shell with olive oil. Spread pizza sauce evenly on shell and top with half the cheese. Arrange vegetables on pizza and cover with remaining cheese.
Bake in 600-700F oven (door off, fire on one side) for 3 - 4 minutes. Place on serving platter and let rest for 2-3 minutes before slicing. Drizzle yogurt sauce on each slice.
• *See DVD part 1/Section 10 for more on Veggie Pizza*

7 LAYER "MEXICAN" PIZZA

This crowd-pleasing appetizer pizza is based on that tasty
American invention, the 7 layer "Mexican" dip.

Makes one pizza

11" pizza (made from 8 oz. pizza dough)
½ C your favorite bean dip *or* refried beans
¼ C chopped black olives
1 C shredded cheddar cheese
½ C chopped tomatoes
¼ C chopped scallions
½ C sour cream
½ C chopped avocado
2 T chopped cilantro (optional)

Start a fire in the center of the oven floor. After half an hour of firing, move the burning wood to the center left or center right. This is determined by which side of the oven will be used for baking the pizza (the heat has been stored in the floor beneath the fire; thus, when the pizza is placed on this spot, a better crust will be achieved). Keep the fire burning until the temperature gauge registers at least 550F. Using the ash stick, move the embers to the side of the oven which will be most visible from the outside. You may start baking pizza when the temperature reaches 600F.

Using a brush, sweep ashes toward the fire. Wrap a damp towel around the brush, and mop the oven floor to remove any ash residue and cool the floor somewhat; this will help prevent crusts from being charred by the extreme initial temperature of the oven floor.

Place pizza slightly closer to the oven opening (the tiles there are a little cooler by the door). After 30 seconds, move pizza further into oven, always checking the bottom of the crust. The next pizza (if you're making more than one) can be placed deeper inside the oven. A constant flame 12 - 16" high should be maintained to ensure ample heat to bake the top of the pizza and maintain the temperature of the oven floor.

Spread bean dip evenly over pizza shell. Top with olives, cheese, tomatoes and scallions.

Bake in 600F oven (door off, fire on one side) for 3 - 4 minutes. Before serving, top with sour cream and avocado; sprinkle with cilantro if desired.

• See DVD part 1/Section 3 for more on Pizza

CHICKEN CALZONE

Hearty and satisfying, this makes a wonderful rustic meal

Makes one calzone

11" pizza (made from 8 oz. pizza dough)
olive oil
1 C cooked chicken breast, chopped
1⁄2 C sautéed, sliced yellow onions
1⁄2 C sautéed, sliced mushrooms (shitake or portobello)
2 garlic cloves, chopped
1⁄2 C shredded mozzarella cheese

Start a fire in the center of the oven floor. After half an hour of firing, move the burning wood to the center left or center right. This is determined by which side of the oven will be used for baking the pizza (the heat has been stored in the floor beneath the fire; thus, when the pizza is placed on this spot, a better crust will be achieved). Keep the fire burning until the temperature gauge registers at least 550F. Using the ash stick, move the embers to the side of the oven which will be most visible from the outside. You may start baking pizza when the temperature reaches 600F.

Using a brush, sweep ashes toward the fire. Wrap a damp towel around the brush, and mop the oven floor to remove any ash residue and cool the floor somewhat; this will help prevent crusts from being charred by the extreme initial temperature of the oven floor.

Place calzone slightly closer to the oven opening (the tiles there are a little cooler by the door). A constant flame 12 - 16" high should be maintained to ensure ample heat to bake the top of the calzone and maintain the temperature of the oven floor.

Brush pizza dough with olive oil, leaving a 1" border around edge. Combine remaining ingredients in bowl. Place filling on one half of pizza shell; season with salt and pepper to taste. Fold other half of dough over filling and double-fold edge to seal securely.

Bake in 600F oven (door off, fire on one side), closer to door opening than you would put a pizza, for 4 - 5 minutes. Let rest 5 minutes before serving.

• See DVD part 2/Section 3 for more on Calzone

SPINACH CALZONE

This sure-fire combination of spinach, feta and pine nuts is a hearty and satisfying vegetarian classic

Makes 2 calzones

2 - 11" pizzas (each made from 8 oz. pizza dough)
1 T olive oil
1 T butter
½ C chopped onions
2 garlic cloves, chopped
1 - 6 oz. package frozen chopped spinach, thawed and drained
½ C chicken broth
salt and pepper to taste
¾ C crumbled feta cheese
¾ C shredded mozzarella cheese
¼ C pine nuts
olive oil for brushing

Start a fire in the center of the oven floor. After half an hour of firing, move the burning wood to the center left or center right. This is determined by which side of the oven will be used for baking the pizza (the heat has been stored in the floor beneath the fire; thus, when the pizza is placed on this spot, a better crust will be achieved). Keep the fire burning until the temperature gauge registers at least 550F. Using the ash stick, move the embers to the side of the oven which will be most visible from the outside. You may start baking pizza when the temperature reaches 600-700F.
Using a brush, sweep ashes toward the fire. Wrap a damp towel around the brush, and mop the oven floor to remove any ash residue and cool the floor some-

what; this will help prevent crusts from being charred by the extreme initial temperature of the oven floor.

Place calzone slightly closer to the oven opening (the tiles there are a little cooler by the door). A constant flame 12 - 16" high should be maintained to ensure ample heat to bake the top of the calzone and maintain the temperature of the oven floor.

In a skillet, heat olive oil and butter. Cook onions until translucent. Add garlic and cook for one minute. Add spinach and cook until moisture has evaporated. Add chicken broth and cook again until liquid has evaporated. Season with salt and pepper. Let cool.

When cool, add feta, mozzarella and pine nuts; mix well. (May be prepared ahead and refrigerated until one hour before baking calzones.)

Brush pizza shell with olive oil, leaving a 1" border around edge. Place half the filling on one half of shell; fold other half of dough over filling and double-fold edge to seal securely. Repeat with the second half of filling to make the other calzone.

Bake calzones one at a time in 600-700F oven (door off, fire on one side), closer to door opening than you would put a pizza, for 4 - 5 minutes. Let rest 5 minutes before serving.
• *See DVD part 2/Section 3 for more on Calzone*

BRUNCH

HAZELNUT BISCOTTI

Why wait for a special occasion? These biscotti are great with that first coffee of the day or anytime you're in the mood for a little treat.

Makes 20 biscotti

1 C butter
1 C sugar
3 eggs
1 tsp vanilla extract
1 T grated lemon peel
4 C all-purpose flour (unbleached)
1 T baking powder
1/2 tsp salt
2 C chopped hazelnuts

Start fire in the center of the oven. Keep it burning for 11/2 - 2 hours, maintaining a temperature of 500 - 525F. Let fire burn out. Push embers to one side. Using a long-handled peel or ashpan, shovel embers into large metal pot containing 2" of water. Carefully cover (very hot) pot with lid and remove to a fireproof surface to cool. Brush remaining ashes to one corner of oven floor. Close oven door for 20 - 30 min. Remove door carefully – it will be very hot! Temperature should be about 500F.

In a mixer with paddle attachment, cream butter. Add sugar and mix for 1 minute. Add eggs, one at a time, beating 30 seconds after each addition. Add vanilla and lemon peel.

In a bowl, combine flour, baking powder and salt. Add to butter mixture, mixing until just blended. Add hazelnuts and mix 10 seconds on low speed.

Divide dough into two portions, shaping each into a rectangle 4" wide, 10" long and 1" thick. Place on greased baking sheet.

Bake in 500F oven (door closed, no embers) for about 30 minutes, or until lightly browned. Remove from oven and let cool. Leave oven door off to allow temperature to drop.

Cut biscotti "loaves" into 1" slices. Arrange on baking sheet, cut side down, and bake at approximately 350F (± 50F) until crisp, about 40 minutes.

• See DVD part 2/Section 11 for more on Baking

APFELPFANNKUCHEN
SKILLET APPLE PANCAKE

Try this morning treat with just a light drift of powdered sugar on top

2 C all purpose flour
1 tsp baking powder
1/2 tsp baking soda
1/2 tsp salt
1 1/2 tsp cinnamon
1/2 C sugar
2 eggs
1/2 C buttermilk
1 tsp vanilla extract
1/2 C melted butter
2 tart apples, grated

Start fire in the center of the oven. Keep it burning for 1 1/2 - 2 hours, maintaining a temperature of 500 - 525F. Let fire burn out. Push embers to one side. Using a long-handled peel or ashpan, shovel embers into large metal pot containing 2" of water. Carefully cover (very hot) pot with lid and remove to a fireproof surface to cool. Brush remaining ashes to one corner of oven floor. Close oven door for 20 - 30 min. Remove door carefully – it will be very hot! Let temperature drop to about 450F.

Sift flour, baking powder, baking soda, salt and cinnamon in mixing bowl. In separate bowl, combine sugar, eggs, vanilla and buttermilk. Pour wet mixture into flour mixture and blend until incorporated. Fold in melted butter and grated apples. Pour batter into a well-buttered (or nonstick) 12" skillet.

Bake in center of 450F oven (door closed, no embers) for 10 - 15 minutes.

• See DVD part 2/Section 11 for more on Baking

LEEK TART

A perfect brunch starter course, or pair this savory dish with a salad for an elegant lunch

1 pie crust*, chilled (recipe follows)
2 C leeks, white part only, cut in 1" lengths
3 T butter
½ tsp freshly ground pepper, and salt to taste
4 eggs
2 C milk
1 C diced cooked ham
¼ tsp freshly grated nutmeg
Or buy ready-made unsweetened pastry crust at any good market.

Start fire in the center of the oven. Keep it burning for 1½ - 2 hours, maintaining a temperature of 500 - 525F. Let fire burn out. Push embers against walls. Brush any remaining ashes to one corner of oven floor. Close oven door for 20 - 30 min. Remove door carefully – it will be very hot! Let temperature drop to about 450F.

Placed chilled dough between 2 sheets of wax paper and roll out to 1/8" thickness, and 1" diameter larger than 10" tart pan. Drape dough over rolling pin and transfer to tart pan. Gently press dough into place, doubling over edge to form rim. Crimp edge using fingers or a small spoon. With a fork, prick dough all over to prevent crust from bubbling. Refrigerate dough for 30 minutes or more.

Slice leek pieces in half lengthwise and rinse thoroughly in cold water to remove any grit; drain well. Melt butter in skillet and cook leeks over low heat until they are translucent. Sprinkle with pepper and salt.

In a mixing bowl, beat together eggs and milk. Add in ham, leeks and nutmeg; stir to combine. Line tart shell with foil and fill with pie weights, dried beans or rice.

Place weighted tart shell in 450F oven (door closed, embers against walls) and bake for about 5 minutes. Remove foil and weights, and bake another 5 minutes. Crust should be dry, but not colored. Pour egg mixture into tart shell and bake for about 15 minutes, or until knife inserted in tart comes out clean.

PIE CRUST
2 C all-purpose flour
½ tsp salt
1 stick cold butter, cut in 1/2" pieces
1 egg
3 T water

In a food processor, pulse dry ingredients together. Add chilled butter and pulse until butter is pea-sized. Add egg and water, and pulse just until combined. The dough should not form a ball while mixing.

Shape dough into a ball by hand. Lightly flour dough and place between two pieces of plastic wrap. With rolling pin, flatten dough to a 6" circle, using additional flour as necessary to prevent sticking. Refrigerate dough for 20-30 minutes before using.

• See DVD part 2/Section 9 for more on Tarts

PIZZA BENEDICT

You'll love this casual, yet impressive interpretation of a brunch classic.

Makes one pizza

11" pizza (made from 8 oz. pizza dough)
1 C shredded mozzarella cheese
4 slices Canadian bacon
4 small eggs
1⁄2 C chopped black olives
Hollandaise sauce (recipe follows)

Start a fire in the center of the oven floor. After half an hour of firing, move the burning wood to the center left or center right. This is determined by which side of the oven will be used for baking the pizza (the heat has been stored in the floor beneath the fire; thus, when the pizza is placed on this spot, a better crust will be achieved). Keep the fire burning until the temperature gauge registers at least 550F. Using the ash stick, move the embers to the side of the oven which will be most visible from the outside. You may start baking pizza when the temperature reaches 600-700F.

Using a brush, sweep ashes toward the fire. Wrap a damp towel around the brush, and mop the oven floor to remove any ash residue and cool the floor somewhat; this will help prevent crusts from being charred by the extreme initial temperature of the oven floor.

Place pizza slightly closer to the oven opening (the tiles there are a little cooler by the door). After 30 seconds, move pizza further into oven, always checking the bottom of the crust. The next pizza (if you're making more than one) can be placed

deeper inside the oven. A constant flame 12 - 16" high should be maintained to ensure ample heat to bake the top of the pizza and maintain the temperature of the oven floor.

Parbake pizza shell until bottom is lightly browned and top is dry, about 2 minutes.

HOLLANDAISE SAUCE
2 T butter
1 T cornstarch
1⁄2 C milk
1 egg yolk
1 tsp lemon juice
salt and pepper to taste

To make Hollandaise: Melt butter in small saucepan. Add cornstarch and whisk for 1 minute over low heat. Add milk. Stirring continuously, add egg yolks; whisk for 1 more minute. Add lemon juice and season to taste with salt and pepper. Keep warm, but do not allow to boil.

Arrange Canadian bacon slices evenly on pizza shell, leaving approximately 1 1⁄2" edge. Spread cheese evenly over top of pizza. Form a little "wall" of cheese around each bacon slice to hold the egg. Gently break an egg onto each slice. Bake in 600-700F oven (door off, fire on one side) until egg whites are just beginning to turn white and eggs are cooked, approximately 2 minutes. Spoon warm Hollandaise Sauce over each egg and sprinkle with chopped olives. Slice and serve.

• See DVD part 1/Section 3 for more on Pizza

BREAKFAST PIZZA

When entertaining weekend guests, that's the time to take full advantage of your oven. After you've used it to cook dinner Saturday night, close the door and the oven will still be warm on Sunday morning. Why not make a small fire and start the day with Breakfast Pizzas? There'll still be enough heat leftover afterward to make a roast for lunch!

Makes one pizza

11" pizza (made from 8 oz. pizza dough)
olive oil
½ C precooked Italian sausage, crumbled
¼ C precooked bacon, crumbled
2 eggs, beaten
1 C shredded mozzarella
½ tsp freshly ground black pepper

Start a fire in the center of the oven floor. After half an hour of firing, move the burning wood to the center left or center right. This is determined by which side of the oven will be used for baking the pizza (the heat has been stored in the floor beneath the fire; thus, when the pizza is placed on this spot, a better crust will be achieved). Keep the fire burning until the temperature gauge registers at least 550F. Using the ash stick, move the embers to the side of the oven which will be most visible from the outside. You may start baking pizza when the temperature reaches 600-700F. Using a brush, sweep ashes toward the fire. Wrap a damp towel around the brush, and mop the oven floor to remove any ash residue and cool the floor somewhat; this will help prevent crusts from being charred by the extreme initial temperature of the oven floor.

Place pizza slightly closer to the oven opening (the tiles there are a little cooler by the door). After 30 seconds, move pizza further into oven, always checking the bottom of the crust. The next pizza (if you're making more than one) can be placed deeper inside the oven. A constant flame 12 - 16" high should be maintained to ensure ample heat to bake the top of the pizza and maintain the temperature of the oven floor.

Brush pizza shell with olive oil. Combine all remaining ingredients in a bowl and pour onto pizza shell.

Bake in 600-700F oven (door off, fire on one side) for 3 - 4 minutes, or until egg is cooked. Let rest 1-2 minutes, then slice and serve.

• *See DVD part 1/Section 3 for more on Pizza*

FISH and SEAFOOD

SEARED TUNA STEAKS with BEET and FRISEE SALAD

These tuna steaks may be oven-seared in a heavy cast iron or stainless steel skillet, or if you prefer you can use the grill.

Serves 4

4 tuna steaks, 3/4" thick
2 T olive oil
1 tsp kosher salt
1 tsp freshly ground black pepper
1 bunch frisee lettuce, torn into bite-sized pieces
1 C julienned cooked red beets
Vinaigrette (recipe follows)

TO SEAR

Start a fire in the center of the oven floor. After half an hour of firing, move the burning wood to the center left or center right. Keep the fire burning until the temperature gauge registers at least 550F. Using the ash stick, move the embers to the side of the oven which will be most visible from the outside. You may start searing when the temperature reaches 600F.

Rub fish with olive oil; season with salt and pepper. Heat a skillet (large enough to hold all steaks) in 600F oven (fire to one side, door off) for 5 minutes or more. Place steaks in preheated skillet and return to oven for 3 minutes. Turn steaks and return to oven until internal temperature reaches 90F, or to taste. ***Do not overcook.***

TO GRILL

Start a fire in the center of the oven. Keep fire burning for 45 minutes to 1 hour. Make sure you have enough embers to grill fish.

Spread embers on the floor of oven slightly larger than the size of the grill. Burning logs can be pushed to one side. Slide grill over embers and preheat for 5 minutes. Pull grill out and, using a clean rag or paper towel, lubricate grate with olive oil. Place items to be grilled on grate and slide back over embers.

Rub fish with olive oil; season with salt and pepper. Place steaks on grill and return to oven for 3 minutes. Turn steaks and return to oven until internal temperature reaches 90F, or to taste. ***Do not overcook.***

VINAIGRETTE

1 T wine vinegar
2 T olive oil
1 T lemon juice
1 garlic clove, pressed
1 T Dijon mustard
salt & pepper to taste

Whisk all vinaigrette ingredients together until emulsified.

Toss lettuce and beets with vinaigrette. Divide salad evenly among four plates. Place a tuna steak on top of each and serve.

• See DVD part 1/Section 4 for more on Grilling

MACADAMIA-CRUSTED SALMON

This rich, crunchy topping goes beautifully with salmon, and the cool, creamy dill sauce brings the whole dish together. A perfect entree for your next dinner party!

Serves 10-12

1 salmon filet, 2-3 lbs.
1 T fresh lemon juice
salt and pepper to taste
pinch of thyme

MARINADE
3 T olive oil
1 tsp Dijon mustard
1 T fresh lemon juice
1 T Pastis, or other anise liqueur
½ tsp hot (red pepper) sauce, or to taste
1 T vinegar

TOPPING
2 T sesame seeds
2 T chopped macadamia nuts

Cucumber Dill Sauce (recipe follows)

Wash salmon filet and pat dry; cut salmon in portions approximately 3" wide. Place in ovenproof ceramic dish. Sprinkle with lemon juice, salt, pepper and thyme. Combine marinade ingredients and pour over salmon. Sprinkle with sesame seeds. Cover dish with plastic wrap and refrigerate 4 hours or overnight.

Allow fish to return to room temperature for one hour before baking.

Start a fire in the center of the oven floor. After half an hour of firing, move the burning wood to the center left or center right. Keep the fire burning until the temperature gauge registers at least 550F. Using the ash stick, move the embers to the side of the oven which will be most visible from the outside. You may start baking when the temperature reaches 600-700F.

Warm baking dish near oven door for 1 minute, then place inside 600F oven across from the fire (as for pizza) for 8-10 minutes. Sprinkle with macadamia nuts, rotate dish and return to oven for 2 - 3 more minutes, or until internal temperature of fish reaches 120-125F (fish will continue to cook in the hot dish). *Do not overcook.*

Serve immediately with Cucumber Dill Sauce.
• *See DVD part 2/Section 4 for more on Salmon Filet*

CUCUMBER DILL SAUCE
6 T sour cream
1 T mayonnaise
2 T fresh lemon juice
2 T fresh dill, chopped
1 medium (or 2 pickling) cucumbers, seeded and grated
¼ tsp salt

Combine all dill sauce ingredients together in a small bowl.

MARINATED HALIBUT STEAKS

The mild flavor of halibut is nicely complemented by this typically Provençal marinade

Serves 2

2 halibut steaks, 1½" thick
juice of ½ lemon
salt and pepper to taste

MARINADE
2 T olive oil
1 tsp Dijon mustard
1 tsp Pastis, or other anise liqueur
(such as Pernod or Ricard)
¼ C white wine
2 T chopped shallots
1 tsp chopped garlic

chopped parsley and lemon wedges for
garnish

Rinse steaks and pat dry. Place in oven-proof baking dish. Squeeze lemon over fish and sprinkle with salt and pepper.

In small bowl or cup, mix marinade ingredients. Pour mixture over halibut steaks; marinate in refrigerator for 3-4 hours or overnight.

Remove baking dish from refrigerator 1 hour before oven roasting.

Start a fire in the center of the oven floor. After half an hour of firing, move the burning wood to the center left or center right. Keep the fire burning until the temperature gauge registers at least 550F. Using the ash stick, move the embers to the side of the oven which will be most visible from the outside. You may start roasting when the temperature reaches 600-700F.

Warm baking dish near oven door for 1 minute, then place inside oven across from the fire (as for pizza) for about 10 minutes (internal temperature should be 120-125F – fish will continue to cook in dish while resting). *Do not overcook.*

Garnish with chopped parsley and lemon wedges, and serve.
• *See DVD part 2/Section 4 for more on Baking Seafood*

POISSON au GRATIN

Good, old fashioned French comfort food, like your grandmother used to make! A true classic that never goes out of style.

Serves 2

1 lb. filets of sole
2 T butter + 1 T for buttering dish
2 T chopped shallots
2 T chopped parsley
1 T chopped garlic
½ C chopped button mushrooms
½ tsp salt
½ tsp freshly ground black pepper
½ C white wine
½ C bread crumbs

Start a fire in the center of the oven floor. After half an hour of firing, move the burning wood to the center left or center right. Keep the fire burning until the temperature gauge registers at least 550F.

Using the ash stick, move the embers to the side of the oven which will be most visible from the outside. You may start baking when the temperature is between 500-600F.

Butter an ovenproof ceramic dish large enough to hold fish filets in a single layer. Arrange fish in dish and top each filet with a piece of butter. Sprinkle all with shallots, parsley, garlic, mushrooms, salt and pepper. Pour wine over fish and cover with breadcrumbs.

Bake in 500-600F oven (door off, fire on) until top is nicely browned and fish is flaky and just cooked through, approximately 15 minutes. *Do not overcook.*

• See DVD part 2/Section 4 for more on Baking Seafood

OVEN ROASTED MUSSELS

Roasting imparts an added bit of concentrated depth and flavor to this variation on the classic moules mariniere.

Serves 2 as a first course or 1 as an entree

2 lbs. fresh mussels
1 T olive oil
1 T butter
3 shallots, or 1⁄2 yellow onion, chopped
1 garlic clove, finely chopped
1⁄2 tsp dried thyme
1⁄2 tsp freshly ground black pepper
1⁄2 C bottled clam juice
1 T Pastis, or other anise liqueur
1⁄2 C white wine
1⁄2 C cream

Start a fire in the center of the oven floor. After half an hour of firing, move the burning wood to the center left or center right. Keep the fire burning until the temperature gauge registers at least 550F. Using the ash stick, move the embers to the side of the oven which will be most visible from the outside. You may start roasting when the temperature reaches 600-700F.

Wash and remove beards from mussels. Arrange in ovenproof ceramic dish.

In small skillet, heat olive oil and butter. Cook shallots until translucent and very soft. Add garlic and cook 1 minute more. Add thyme, pepper, clam juice, Pastis, wine and cream. Boil for 2 minutes. Keep warm.

Place mussels in 600 - 700F oven, as you would for pizza (fire on, door off), until all mussels are open, 1 to 2 minutes. Discard any unopened mussels. Remove from oven, pour sauce over mussels, and serve with garlic bread.

• *See DVD part 2/Section 5 for more on Roasted Mussels*

COQUILLES ST. JACQUES

Because this old-school classic can be prepared entirely in advance, it's the ideal dish for easy (yet elegant) entertaining.

Serves 6 as a first course

6 scallop shells,* or 6 small gratin dishes
2 T butter
1 T olive oil
3 T chopped shallots or onion
½ tsp salt
½ tsp white pepper
1 C chopped white mushrooms
1 T flour
½ C white wine
1 C cream
12 oz. scallops (keep 6 whole and chop the rest)
½ C bread crumbs
½ C grated mozzarella
rock salt

Scallop shells can be purchased online from Williams Sonoma or other gourmet suppliers.

Start a fire in the center of the oven floor. After half an hour of firing, move the burning wood to the center left or center right. Keep the fire burning until the temperature gauge registers at least 550F. Using the ash stick, move the embers to the side of the oven which will be most visible from the outside. You may start baking when the temperature reaches 600-700F.

Heat butter and oil in 10" skillet. Add shallots and cook at low heat until translucent. Sprinkle with salt and pepper. Add mushrooms and stir for 1 minute. Sprinkle flour over mixture and stir for 1 minute more. Add wine and cream; bring to boil and cook for 2 minutes, stirring constantly. Add scallops and cook for 1 minute.

Fill shells with scallop mixture and top each with one whole scallop. Evenly distribute bread crumbs and grated cheese atop all the shells. Place shells on baking sheet or ovenproof dish that's been covered with ½" of rock salt (this is to stabilize shells). (May be prepared to this point 4 - 5 hours ahead of time and refrigerated. Let stand at room temperature for 30 minutes before baking.)

Warm baking dish near oven door for 1 minute, then place inside 600-700F oven across from the fire (as for pizza) for 4 to 5 minutes, or until cheese is melted and top is nicely browned. (Or may be baked in 500 - 600F oven if preferred (no fire, door closed, embers against walls), for 7 to 10 minutes. *Do not overcook.*
• *See DVD part 2/Section 4 for more on Baking Seafood*

STUFFED LOBSTER TAILS

While this dish requires a bit more preparation than some of the others, the results are well worth it

Serves 6

4 T salt
1 C chopped carrots
1 stalk celery, chopped
1 onion, quartered
bouquet garni (4 sprigs parsley, 4 sprigs thyme, 1 bay leaf)
6 lobster tails
1⁄2 C butter
1⁄4 C flour
11⁄2 C half & half
1 tsp lemon zest
1 T lemon juice
1 tsp paprika
2 eggs, separated
salt and pepper to taste
rock salt
1⁄2 C mozzarella cheese, shredded

Start a fire in the center of the oven floor. After half an hour of firing, move the burning wood to the center left or center right. Keep the fire burning until the temperature gauge registers at least 550F. Using the ash stick, move the embers to the side of the oven which will be most visible from the outside. You may start baking when the temperature reaches 550-600F.

Bring 6 quarts of water to boil with salt, carrots, celery, onion and bouquet garni. Add lobster tails and cook for 20 minutes, or until internal temperature reaches 120F.

Remove lobster and immediately plunge into ice water to avoid overcooking. Carefully remove lobster meat, keeping shells intact. Chop meat in 1⁄2" dice and set aside.

Melt butter in saucepan. Stir in flour and mix until smooth. Gradually add half & half, stirring constantly. Cook just until mixture boils and is thickened. Add lemon zest, juice and paprika.

Beat egg yolks. Stir 1/4 cup of cream mixture into yolks to temper. Add all of tempered yolk mixture back into sauce and cook 2 minutes, stirring constantly. Season with salt and pepper.

Spread rock salt 1⁄2" thick on baking sheet. Combine reserved lobster meat with half of sauce and distribute evenly among shells. Arrange shells on salt bed to keep them in place. Melt cheese in remaining sauce; mix well.

Beat egg whites until soft peaks form. Fold into cheese sauce and spoon over lobster shells, covering contents completely.

Warm baking dish near oven door for 1 minute, then place inside 600-700F oven across from the fire (as for pizza) for 4 to 5 minutes, or until cheese is melted and top is nicely browned. (Or may be baked in 500 - 600F oven if preferred (no fire, door closed, embers against walls), for 7 to 10 minutes. *Do not overcook.*
• *See DVD part 2/Section 4 for more on Baking Seafood*

WHOLE FISH in SALT CRUST

This dish couldn't be easier to prepare, but the dramatic effect when you crack open the crust will delight and impress your guests – and surprisingly, the taste isn't salty at all!

Serves 6-8

1 - 3 lb whole fish, such as salmon, pink trout or white fish, about 17" long
2 T olive oil
freshly ground pepper
1 lemon, cut into 1/8" thick slices
1 fennel bulb, cut into 1/8" thick slices
2 sprigs parsley
1 tsp dried thyme, or 2 tsp fresh
6 large leaves of Romaine lettuce, blanched and patted dry
4 C rock salt
3 T flour
4 T water
4 lemon wedges (for garnish)

Start a fire in the center of the oven floor. After half an hour of firing, move the burning wood to the center left or center right. Keep the fire burning until the temperature gauge registers at least 550F. Using the ash stick, move the embers to the side of the oven which will be most visible from the outside. Allow the temperature to continue rising; you may start baking when the temperature reaches 600-700F.

Wash fish and pat dry. Rub inside and out with olive oil, and season with pepper. Fill fish cavity with sliced lemon, fennel, parsley and thyme. Wrap fish in lettuce leaves (tail may be left exposed)

Generously butter a large ovenproof platter. In large bowl, combine salt, flour and water to create a paste. Place fish on platter and cover completely with a layer of salt mixture about 1/4" thick, keeping the fish's shape to the extent possible. Insert temperature probe in thickest part of fish, leaving gauge outside oven while baking.

Bake in 600 - 700F oven using pizza fire (door off, across from fire) for 20 minutes. *Or,* may be baked in 550F oven (no flame, door closed, embers against walls) for 30 minutes. Fish is done when internal temperature registers 120-125F. *Do not overcook.*

Crack salt and remove crust, then carefully remove lettuce leaves. Serve fish from platter, or transfer to another serving dish. Garnish with lemon wedges.
• *See DVD part 2/Section 4 for more on Baking Seafood*

SEA BASS en PAPILLOTE

This dish makes a beautiful presentation when the packets are snipped open at the table and the delicious contents revealed. Be sure to julienne the vegetables uniformly, about 1/8" thick and 3" long.

Serves 4

1 leek, julienned (white part only)
1 small carrot, julienned
1 fennel bulb, thinly sliced
2 cloves garlic, chopped
2 sprigs parsley, chopped
½ tsp dried thyme
1 T capers
1 T butter
1 T olive oil

4 sea bass filets*, 4 to 6 oz. each
4 - 12" x 12" pieces of parchment paper *OR* aluminum foil
salt and pepper to taste
½ stick butter, cut into small pieces
4 T fresh lemon juice
4 T white wine
other firm, white fleshed fish such as halibut, trout, etc. can be substituted.

Start a fire in the center of the oven floor. After half an hour of firing, move the burning wood to the center left or center right. Keep the fire burning until the temperature gauge registers at least 550F. Using the ash stick, move the embers to the side of the oven which will be most visible from the outside. Allow the temperature to continue rising; you may start baking when the temperature reaches 600-700F.

Heat butter and olive oil in a skillet. Saute vegetables, garlic, capers and herbs over medium heat until vegetables are crisp-tender; set aside.

Place 1 fish filet on lower half of each piece of foil or parchment; season with salt and pepper. Evenly distribute cooked vegetable mixture over each filet. Dot with butter and drizzle with lemon juice and wine.
Fold parchment or foil over fish and crimp all edges, tucking under. Seal well.

Make a small slit in top of each packet, and bake on floor of 600 - 700F oven using a pizza fire (door off, across from fire) for 8 to 10 minutes, *or* may alternately be cooked at 500F (no fire, door closed, embers against walls) for 10 to 12 minutes. Fish is done when internal temperature registers 120-125F. *Do not overcook.*
• *See DVD part 2/Section 4 for more on Baking Seafood*

HOT SMOKED SALMON

I like to serve this fish with potatoes and a simple green salad. Cucumber Dill Sauce (pg. 69) goes especially well with it.

Serves 6-8

1 2 lb. salmon filet
2 T fresh lemon juice
1 T Pastis, or other anise liqueur
2 T olive oil
salt and pepper to taste
½ T dried thyme
1 C white wine

3 medium carrots
1 celery rib
1 fennel bulb, cut into 3 pieces
2 leeks, sliced in half lengthwise
1 yellow onion, quartered

1C alder chips, soaked in water for 15 minutes

Start a fire in the center of the oven floor. Keep the fire burning until the temperature gauge registers at least 550F. Using the ash stick, move the embers against the oven walls. You may start baking when the temperature reaches 500F.

Wash salmon filet and pat dry. Combine lemon juice and Pastis. Rub both sides of fish with lemon juice mixture, olive oil, salt, pepper and thyme.

In an ovenproof shallow roasting pan or dish, make a bed for the fish using the cut vegetables. Place fish on top and pour wine into pan.

Sprinkle the soaked alder chips on hot embers. Slide fish to center of 500F oven (door closed, embers against walls) for 20 - 30 minutes or until internal temperature of fish reaches 120-125F. *Do not overcook.*

NOTE: The intensity of the smoke flavor may be adjusted by leaving the door slightly open to allow some of the smoke to escape.

• *See DVD part 1/Section 14 for more on Baking Salmon*

POULTRY

COQ au VIN

As a child, when we had family over for a special Sunday dinner, we cooked a large rooster ("coq") in red wine. In winter, my mother made this classic French country dish using rabbit instead; see pg. 98 for this recipe variation.

Serves 4-6

1 3½ - 4 lb. chicken, cut into pieces
1 tsp salt
1 tsp freshly ground pepper
2 T flour
1 T olive oil
2 T butter
2 C sliced mushrooms (white mushrooms are fine, but shitaki, chanterelle or porcini are better)
1 C chopped onion (or 1 C pearl onions, peeled)
2 cloves crushed garlic
1 C red wine
1 C chicken stock
1 T tomato paste
bouquet garni (2 sprigs parsley, 1 bay leaf, 2 springs fresh thyme – tied with string)
2 T chopped parsley for garnish

Start a fire in the center of the oven floor. Keep the fire burning until the temperature gauge registers at least 550F. Using the ash stick, move the embers against the oven walls. You may start baking when the temperature reaches 550F.

Season chicken pieces with salt and pepper. In heavy enameled or metal roasting pan, heat oil and butter in a 500-550F oven (no fire, embers against walls). When oil is very hot, add chicken pieces and brown on all sides, 2 - 3 minutes on each side. Remove chicken from pan. Using same pan, saute mushrooms and onions for 2 minutes. Add flour and mix for 1 minute. Return chicken to pan together with remaining ingredients (except parsley). Cover and roast chicken for about 30 minutes. Remove lid and continue roasting another 10 minutes until chicken is tender.

Adjust seasoning to taste. Sprinkle with chopped parsley and serve.

• *See DVD part 1/Section 13 for more on Roasting*

GRILLED BALSAMIC CHICKEN BREASTS

Not only are these an easy and tasty main course, they make terrific sandwiches. Toast pain au levain slices, spread them with Dijon mustard and top with chicken, roasted bell peppers and arugula. Delicious!

Serves 2

2 half chicken breasts

MARINADE
1 small onion, sliced
juice and zest of 1 lemon
1 T fresh rosemary, or ½ T dried
2 T fresh thyme, or 1 T dried
1 T balsamic vinegar
½ C olive oil
1 T Dijon mustard

Salt and pepper to taste

Combine marinade ingredients; pour over chicken in shallow glass baking dish or resealable food storage bag and marinate for 4 hours in refrigerator.

One hour before grilling, remove chicken from refrigerator.

Meanwhile, start a fire in the center of the oven. Keep fire burning for 45 minutes to 1 hour. Make sure you have enough embers to grill chicken pieces.

Spread embers on the floor of oven slightly larger than the size of the grill. Burning logs can be pushed to one side. Slide grill over embers and preheat for 5 minutes. Pull grill out and, using a clean rag or paper towel, lubricate grate with olive oil. Place items to be grilled on grate and slide back over embers.

On well-oiled, hot grill, cook chicken until it reaches internal temperature of 165-170F, approximately 10-15 minutes. Add salt and pepper to taste.
• *See DVD part 1/Section 4 for more on Grilling*

CHICKEN KEBABS

More tender, flavorful and juicy than you'd expect – I think this method makes kebabs that are far superior to any regular backyard grill

Serves 4-6

1½ lbs. skinless, boneless chicken breasts
½ tsp kosher salt
freshly ground black pepper

MARINADE
¼ C olive oil
2 T Dijon mustard
1 T lemon juice
1 T wine vinegar
½ tsp dried thyme

Wash and dry chicken breasts. Cut chicken into 1½" cubes. Place in glass bowl, and sprinkle with salt and pepper.

Combine all marinade ingredients. Pour over chicken pieces and turn well. Marinate for 4 hours (or overnight) in refrigerator.

Skewer chicken on metal skewers. (*or*, if using wooden skewers, soak for 10 minutes in water before skewering chicken.) Cover skewered chicken and let rest at room temperature for 30 minutes.

Meanwhile, start a fire in the center of the oven. Keep fire burning for 45 minutes to 1 hour. Make sure you have enough embers to grill kebabs.
Spread embers on the floor of oven slightly larger than the size of the grill. Burning logs can be pushed to one side. Slide grill over embers and preheat for 5 minutes. Pull grill out and, using a clean rag or paper towel, lubricate grate with olive oil. Place items to be grilled on grate and slide back over embers.

Grill skewers for 2 minutes on each side, to internal temperature of 160F.
• *See DVD part 1/Section 4 for more on Grilling*

ROAST DUCK in CRANBERRY-ORANGE SAUCE

Whole ducks can be found in the frozen section of some well-stocked markets, or online from D'Artagnan. When your guests taste this dish, they'll agree it was worth the extra effort of finding the duck!

Serves 4-6

1 4-5 lb. duck
2 T olive oil
1 tsp salt
½ tsp pepper
3 medium carrots
1 stalk celery, cut in 3 pieces
1 medium onion, quartered
zest of ½ orange

CRANBERRY-ORANGE SAUCE
4 T butter
2 T olive oil
¼ C chopped shallots
2 cloves chopped garlic
1 tsp thyme
½ tsp pepper
½ C red wine
1 C chicken stock
juice of ½ orange
zest of ½ orange
½ C cranberries, fresh or frozen
2 T Grand Marnier or Cointreau
1 T cornstarch

Start a fire in the center of the oven floor. Keep the fire burning until the temperature gauge registers at least 550F. Using the ash stick, move the embers against the oven walls. You may start baking when the temperature reaches 500F.

Rinse duck in cold water and pat dry with paper towels. Season inside and out with salt and pepper, and put orange zest in duck cavity. Arrange carrots, celery and onion at random in roasting pan. Secure legs and wings, and place breast side down on bed of vegetables.

Roast in center of 500F oven (door closed, embers against walls) for 20 minutes. Remove pan and drain off most of the fat. Turn duck over (breast side up) and return to oven for 30 to 40 minutes more, until meat thermometer registers 170F when inserted at thickest part of thigh and breast. Remove duck from oven and let rest, covered loosely with foil, for 10 minutes.

Meanwhile, make sauce. Heat 2T of the butter and olive oil in skillet. Cook shallots for 3 - 4 minutes, until translucent. Add garlic, thyme and pepper; cook 1 minute more. Add wine, all but 1 tablespoon of stock, orange juice and zest, cranberries and Grand Marnier. Dissolve cornstarch in remaining tablespoon of stock and stir into sauce. Simmer mixture until reduced by half.

Strain sauce into saucepan; you should have about 1 cup. Add remaining 2T butter, 1 tablespoon at a time, stirring well after each addition. Do not allow sauce to boil. Serve duck with cranberry-orange sauce.

• See DVD part 1/Section 13 for more on Roasting

ROAST TURKEY

This is an excellent 'master recipe' for roast turkey; once you're comfortable with it, you can easily experiment by adding other spices or sauces.

Serves 10-15 with leftovers

1 15-17 lb. turkey
1 lemon, halved
3 T olive oil
1 T salt
1 T pepper
3 medium carrots
1 rib celery, cut in 3 pieces
1 yellow onion, quartered
4 sprigs parsley
2 leeks, sliced in half lengthwise
4 T butter, softened
1 tsp salt
1 tsp pepper
1 tsp dried thyme
1 C white wine

Start a fire in the center of the oven floor. Keep oven fired for 2-3 hours. After flames subside, move embers against the oven walls. Place item to be roasted in center of oven; close door. Starting temperature for roasting should be 500F.

Rinse turkey well, inside and out, under cold running water; pat dry with paper towels. Rub turkey inside and out with the lemon half (squeezing out juice as you go), then with olive oil. Season inside and out with salt and pepper.

Line a shallow roasting pan with enough heavy gauge foil to seal turkey completely. Arrange vegetables in bottom of pan.

In a small bowl or cup, thoroughly combine butter with salt, pepper and thyme. With your fingers, carefully loosen skin starting at the neck of the bird, continuing to separate the skin from the meat all the way down over the breast (being careful not to tear skin), and pack breast area under skin with butter mixture. Pull neck skin and fasten to back of bird with small skewer. Truss legs together.

Place turkey, breast side up, in pan on vegetable bed. Lock wings in place by tucking tips under. Pour wine in roasting pan. Roll excess foil down on each side so turkey will be exposed for the first 45 minutes of cooking. Insert thermometer in thickest part of thigh, and place turkey in center of 500F oven (door closed, embers against walls).

Check turkey after 20 minutes. If breast is browning too fast, place a double layer of foil over bird. After about 45 minutes, carefully slide roasting pan out of oven. Unroll foil on sides and seal to cover turkey completely. Return to oven for approximately 1½ hours more. Turkey is done when thermometer registers 165-175F.*
Let rest 15-20 minutes before serving.
*Note: Federal food safety guidelines recommend 180F for turkey, but the consensus among cooks is that 180F leaves the bird overcooked to the point of tasting like cardboard. Unless you're cooking for those with compromised immune systems, I recommend the slightly lower internal temperature mentioned above.
• See DVD part 1/Section 13 for more on Roast Turkey

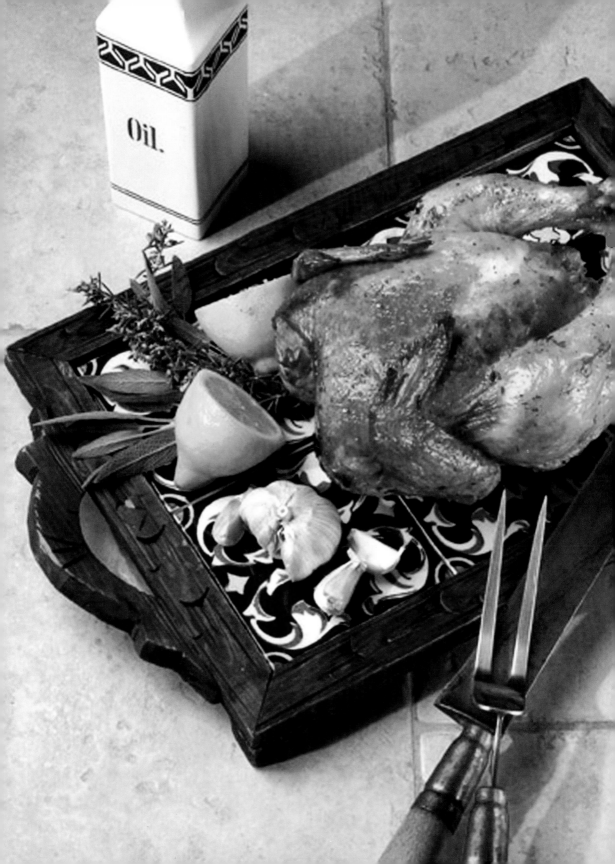

ROAST CHICKEN

I've found that nothing produces a juicier, more evenly cooked roast chicken than a vertical roasting rack. Once you've tried using one, you'll never go back to roasting your chickens any other way.

Serves 4

1 3-4 lb. roasting chicken
1/2 lemon
2 T olive oil
1 tsp salt
1 tsp pepper
1 tsp dried thyme
1 tsp dried rosemary, or 2 tsp fresh
2 T butter
2 + 6 cloves garlic

Start a fire in the center of the oven floor. Keep oven fired for 2 hours. After flames subside, move embers against the oven walls. Place item to be roasted in center of oven; close door. Starting temperature for roasting should be 450-500F.

Rinse chicken well under running water; pat dry. Rub chicken inside and out with the half lemon, squeezing out juice as you go (reserve lemon half for insertion in cavity); then rub with olive oil. Season inside and out with 1/2 teaspoon each of salt, pepper and herbs. Place squeezed lemon half in cavity.

In a small bowl or cup, thoroughly combine butter with remaining salt, pepper, herbs and 2 pressed garlic cloves. With your fingers, carefully loosen skin starting at the neck of the chicken, continuing to separate the skin from the meat all the way down over the breast (being careful not to tear skin), and pack breast area under skin with butter mixture.

Smash remaining 6 whole garlic cloves and place in dish of vertical chicken roaster. Slip chicken onto vertical roasting rack. Secure legs and wings, and tent top of chicken with aluminum foil for first 20 minutes.

Roast in center of 450-500F oven (door closed, embers against walls) for 45-60 minutes, until meat thermometer registers 170F when inserted at thickest part of thigh. Let rest 10-15 minutes before serving.

• See DVD part 1/Section 11 for more on Roast Chicken

MEATS

SEARED FLANK STEAK

*A quick and satisfying weeknight meal, or tasty enough
to serve to weekend guests*

Serves 4-6

1½-2 lbs. flank steak
1 T olive oil
2 T butter
1 tsp salt
1 tsp freshly ground black pepper
1 C sliced shallots or onions
3 garlic cloves, chopped
¼ C red wine
¼ C chicken or beef broth
½ tsp dried thyme

Start a fire in the center of the oven floor.
After half an hour of firing, move the
burning wood to the center left or center
right. Keep the fire burning until the
temperature gauge registers at least 550F.
Using the ash stick, move the embers to
the side of the oven which will be most
visible from the outside. Allow oven
temperature to continue to rise to at least
600F; you may start searing at 600F.

In a 12" skillet, combine olive oil and butter.
Place in a very hot oven (door open, fire on one
side) to melt butter.

Place steak in skillet and sear for at least 2
minutes on each side, depending on thickness.
When meat is cooked (125F internal temperature for medium), transfer to ovenproof serving
dish and keep warm near front door of oven.

Use the same skillet to sauté shallots and garlic,
cooking until translucent. Add wine, broth and
thyme. Cook until liquid is reduced by half.

Slice flank steak across grain and serve with
sauce spooned over.

*• See DVD part 2/Section 4 for more on cooking
across from the fire*

STEAK or LAMB KEBAB

I recommend grilling the vegetables separately. Skewer 2" cubes of eggplant, 2" squares of various colored bell pepper, small whole tomatoes, white mushrooms and quartered onions; brush with olive oil, season with salt and pepper and grill alongside the meat.

Serves 4-6

1½ lbs. top sirloin *or* deboned leg of lamb
½ tsp kosher salt
freshly ground black pepper

MARINADE
¼ C olive oil
2 T tomato paste
1 T Dijon mustard
2 T balsamic vinegar
½ C grated yellow onion
½ tsp dried thyme
½ tsp hot sauce, or to taste
2 cloves crushed garlic

Cut meat into 1½" cubes. Place in glass bowl, and sprinkle with salt and pepper. Combine all marinade ingredients. Pour over meat and turn well. Marinate for 4 hours (or overnight) in refrigerator.

Bring meat to room temperature. Skewer meat on metal skewers. (If using wooden skewers, soak in water for 10 minutes first.)

Meanwhile, start a fire in the center of the oven. Keep fire burning for 45 minutes to 1 hour. Make sure you have enough embers to grill kebabs.

Spread embers on the floor of oven slightly larger than the size of the grill. Burning logs can be pushed to one side. Slide grill over embers and preheat for 5 minutes. Pull grill out and, using a clean rag or paper towel, lubricate grate with olive oil. Place items to be grilled on grate and slide back over embers.

Grill skewers for 2 - 3 minutes on each side, to an internal temperature of 125F for medium rare.

• *See DVD part 1/Section 4 for more on Grilling*

BBQ RIBEYE STEAKS

The hit of your next cookout!

Serves 8-10

6 to 8 ribeye steaks, about ¾" thick
salt, pepper and thyme, to taste

MARINADE
1/4 C olive oil
1 T Dijon mustard
2 T tomato paste
1 T balsamic vinegar
3 T spicy barbecue sauce

1 large yellow onion, thinly sliced and separated into rings

Combine marinade ingredients in bowl; mix well.

Remove all visible fat from the steaks. (If steaks are too thick, pound them down by hand.) Season with salt, pepper and thyme. Brush with marinade.

Layer half the onion rings in bottom of large baking dish; place steaks marinade side down on top of onions. Season with salt, pepper and thyme. Evenly cover with remaining marinade and onion rings. Cover dish with foil or plastic wrap and refrigerate for 4 hours or overnight.

Return steaks to room temperature for 1 hour before grilling.

Meanwhile, start a fire in the center of the oven. Keep fire burning for 45 minutes to 1 hour. Make sure you have enough embers to grill steaks.

Spread embers on the floor of oven slightly larger than the size of the grill. Burning logs can be pushed to one side. Slide grill over embers and preheat for 5 minutes. Pull grill out and, using a clean rag or paper towel, lubricate grate with olive oil.

Arrange steaks on preheated, lubricated grill and return grill to oven. Turn meat after 2 minutes. Total cooking time should be about 5 minutes for medium rare (125F), or to your taste. *Do not overcook.* Allow steaks to rest 3 to 4 minutes before serving.

• See DVD part 1/Section 4 for more on Grilling

BBQ SHORT RIBS

The main prep for these ribs can be done the day before, and then barbecued just before serving.
Larger racks of ribs (like pork or beef) may be prepared the same way.

Serves 4–6

6 lbs. bone-in beef short ribs
4 C beef broth
4 C water
1 onion, quartered
1 C chopped carrots
1/2 C chopped celery
bouquet garni (2 sprigs fresh thyme, 2 bay
leaves; 3 sprigs parsley, tied in a bundle)
1 T peppercorns

1 C your favorite BBQ sauce, *or* mix together the following:
1/4 C olive oil
2 T balsamic vinegar
1 T hot sauce
1/2 tsp freshly ground black pepper
1/2 tsp salt
2 T Dijon mustard
2 T tomato paste
2 cloves crushed garlic

In large oval pot, combine ribs with all
ingredients (except BBQ sauce). Bring to
a boil over medium heat. Reduce heat to low
and simmer until ribs are tender, about 1 hour.
Remove ribs and pat dry. (May be refrigerated
overnight, if desired. Return ribs to room temperature before barbecuing.) Brush ribs with
barbecue sauce.

Meanwhile, start a fire in the center of the
oven. Keep fire burning for 45 minutes to 1
hour. Make sure you have enough embers to
grill ribs.

Spread embers on the floor of oven slightly
larger than the size of the grill. Burning logs
can be pushed to one side. Slide grill over
embers and preheat for 5 minutes. Pull grill
out and, using a clean rag or paper towel, lubricate grate with olive oil. Place items to be
grilled on grate and slide back over embers.

Grill over hot coals until nicely colored, about 2
minutes on each side. Place ribs on platter and
brush with barbecue sauce once more before
serving.
• *See DVD part 1/Section 4 for more on Grilling*

BONELESS ROAST LEG of LAMB

Following are two very useful "master recipes" for leg of lamb. This one is for cooking a boneless leg, and the one on the opposite page is for bone-in. Once you've mastered the techniques, you can experiment all you like with other spices and marinades.

Serves 6-8

1 4 lb. boneless leg of lamb
¼ C chopped fresh basil
¼ C chopped fresh oregano
1 T chopped fresh thyme, or 1 tsp dried
2 cloves garlic, chopped
1 tsp salt
1 tsp freshly ground pepper
2 T olive oil

additional olive oil, salt & pepper for outside of leg

Start a fire in the center of the oven floor. Keep oven fired for 2 hours. After flames subside, move embers against the oven walls. Place item to be roasted in center of oven; close door. Starting temperature for roasting should be 500F.

Open leg of lamb. Combine all ingredients well and spread evenly on inside of leg. Roll leg back up. Rub outside of lamb with olive oil and season with salt and pepper.

Place roast, fat side up, on V-rack in shallow roasting pan. Pour 1 cup water in bottom of pan to prevent drippings from smoking.

Roast in 500F oven (door closed, embers against walls) for 1¼-1¾ hours, or until internal temperature registers 125F. Remove from oven, tent with foil and let rest for 15 minutes before carving. Internal temperature will continue to rise to 140F (medium rare) after resting.

NOTE: If top browns too fast, cover roast with double layer of foil for first ½ hour.

• *See DVD part 2/Section 10 for more on Leg of Lamb*

ROAST LEG of LAMB

Serves 6-8

1 4-5 lb. leg of lamb, bone-in
2 cloves garlic, slivered
3 T olive oil
1 T chopped fresh rosemary, or 1 tsp dried
1 T chopped fresh thyme, or 1 tsp dried
1 tsp salt
1 tsp freshly ground pepper

Start a fire in the center of the oven floor. Keep oven fired for 2 hours. After flames subside, move embers against the oven walls. Place item to be roasted in center of oven; close door. Starting temperature for roasting should be 500F.

Cut 6 - 8 3⁄4" slits in meaty part of lamb; insert a sliver of garlic in each. Combine olive oil with herbs and spices; rub on lamb.

Place roast on V-rack in shallow roasting pan. Pour 1 cup water in bottom of pan to prevent drippings from smoking.

Roast in 500F oven (door closed, embers against walls) for 1¼-1¾ hours, or until internal temperature registers 125F. Remove from oven, tent with foil and let rest for 15 minutes before carving. Internal temperature will continue to rise to 140F (medium rare) after resting.

NOTE: If top browns too fast, cover roast with double layer of foil for first 1⁄2 hour.
• *See DVD part 2/Section 10 for more on Leg of Lamb*

BOEUF BOURGUIGNON

Beef stew as they prepare it in Burgundy - a true country classic

Serves 6-8

3 lbs. beef chuck *or* bottom round, cut into
2" cubes

MARINADE
3 onions, quartered
2 carrots, sliced
1 leek, white part only, chopped
1 rib celery, sliced
1/2 tsp black peppercorns
1 bottle red wine

5 T olive oil
2 T tomato paste
1/4 C flour
2 cloves garlic, minced
1 C beef or chicken stock
bouquet garni (2 thyme springs, 1 bay leaf,
2 sprigs parsley, tied in cheesecloth)
3 C sliced mushrooms

In large glass bowl, combine marinade
ingredients; add beef and turn well.
Marinate overnight in refrigerator.

Remove beef from marinade; pat dry
with paper towels. Strain and reserve
marinade liquid.

Meanwhile, start a fire in the center of
the oven floor. Keep oven fired for 2
hours. After flames subside, move embers against the oven walls. Place item to be
roasted in center of oven; close door. Starting temperature for roasting should be 550F.

In heavy enamel or metal roasting pan, heat 2
tablespoons of the oil in 550F oven (no flame,
embers against walls). When oil is very hot,
add half the meat and saute until browned on
all sides, 2 to 3 minutes. Remove meat and set
aside. Add another 2 tablespoons of oil and
cook remaining meat.

With all beef in roasting pan, add tomato paste
and sprinkle with flour. Mix well and return to
oven for 2 minutes, stirring twice. Add reserved
marinade, garlic, stock and bouquet garni.
Cover with foil (or lid) and cook in oven with
door closed for about 2 hours or until meat is
tender. Skim fat from cooking liquid as needed.

Remove meat from roasting pan. Strain sauce
and return to roasting pan. Cook sauce uncovered for 5 - 10 minutes. Adjust seasoning to
taste.

While sauce is reducing, sauté mushrooms in
a skillet with remaining oil for 5 minutes. Add
mushrooms and meat to roasting pan; combine
well. Cook for 10 minutes.

Serve over mashed potatoes, rice or pasta.
• See DVD part 1/Section 13 for more on Roasting

ROAST RABBIT (MY MOTHER'S "LAPIN au VIN")

While not commonly eaten in America, rabbit is a great favorite in France. You can find frozen rabbit at some well stocked markets, or online at exoticmeats.com.

Serves 4-6

1 3-4 lb. rabbit

MARINADE
2 T tomato paste
¼ C olive oil
2 T balsamic vinegar
1 C red wine
1 C chicken stock
bouquet garni (1 bay leaf, 2 sprigs parsley, 1 sprig thyme, tied together)

1 tsp salt
½ tsp pepper
2 T flour
2 T butter
2 T olive oil
¼ C chopped shallots
1 T chopped garlic
8 chanterelles or porcini mushrooms
½ tsp dried thyme

Wash and dry rabbit; cut into 6 pieces. In a quart jar with a lid, mix tomato paste with olive oil; add vinegar, wine, stock and bouquet garni. Shake to mix well. Place rabbit pieces in a resealable food storage bag and add marinade, coating all pieces well. Refrigerate for 4 hours or overnight, turning the bag 3 or 4 times.

Meanwhile, start a fire in the center of the oven floor. Keep the oven fired for 2 hours. After flames subside, move embers against the oven walls. Place item to be roasted in center of oven; close door. Starting temperature for roasting should be 500F.

Drain rabbit pieces, and save marinade. Discard bouquet garni. Dry rabbit pieces with paper towels, and season with salt and pepper. Sprinkle with flour.

Heat butter and oil in shallow roasting pan (ceramic or cast iron) in hot oven. Saute rabbit pieces in 500F oven for about 1 minute on each side. Add shallots, garlic, mushrooms and thyme to roasting pan, mixing to coat for 1 minute with wooden spoon. Pour reserved marinade over meat and close door. Turn meat every 15 minutes until tender, about 45 minutes. Serve with sauce.

• See DVD part 1/Section 13 for more on Roasting

COCHON de LAIT ROAST SUCKLING PIG

For the more ambitious cook, the woodfired oven is an ideal way to prepare whole roasts such as this one

Serves 12-14

25 lb. suckling pig

BASTING MARINADE
1/2 C olive oil
1/2 C wine vinegar
2 T salt
1 T ground pepper
2 T chopped fresh rosemary
1 T dried thyme

STUFFING
2 T butter
1 C brown rice
11/2 C chicken broth
2 T butter
2 T olive oil
2 C chopped onions
1 C chopped celery
1 C chopped red peppers
1 C chopped pippin apples (unpeeled)
10-oz package uncooked pork sausage
1/2 C chopped fennel bulb
1/4 C apple brandy, such as Calvados
1 C chopped pecans
1 C cooked corn
1/4 C chopped parsley
3 C bread cubes
salt and pepper to taste

Wash pig and pat dry. Whisk marinade ingredients together. Brush pig liberally inside and out with marinade. Marinate 4 hours or overnight.

Meanwhile, start a fire in the center of the oven floor. Keep oven fired for 3-4 hours. After flames subside, move embers against the oven walls. Place item to be roasted in center of oven; close door. Starting temperature for roasting should be 500F.

Melt butter in saucepan. Cook rice for 3-4 minutes, stirring constantly. Add chicken broth and bring to boil. Simmer covered until all liquid is absorbed, about 20 minutes. Remove from heat and let rest for 15 minutes.

In small skillet, cook sausage, breaking it up as it browns; set aside. In large skillet, heat butter and olive oil. Add onions and cook on low heat until translucent. Add celery, peppers, apples, fennel and brandy. Cook, stirring and mixing well, for 15 minutes, or until vegetables are tender. Add pecans, rice, corn, parsley, sausage and bread cubes. Mix well; season with salt and pepper. Let cool.

Fill cavity of pig with stuffing. Double fold skin and close opening using large needle and thread. Refirgerate if not roasting immediately.

Bring roast back to room temperature, if refrigerated. Roast in 500F oven (door closed, embers against walls) for 21/2 - 3 hours, or until internal temperature registers 160F. Remove from oven, tent with foil and let rest for 15 minutes before carving. If top browns too quickly during cooking, cover with a double layer of aluminum foil.

NOTE: Leftover stuffing can be served separately – it tastes great all by itself.
• See DVD part 1/Section 13 for more on Roasting

HERB-CRUSTED RACK of LAMB

Easy to prepare yet so impressive, your guests will think you fussed for hours!

Serves 4-6

2 racks of lamb, 1 1/2 lbs. each
2 cloves garlic, crushed
1 T olive oil
1 T Dijon mustard
1 T balsamic vinegar
1 T dried thyme, or 2 T fresh thyme
1/2 tsp salt
1/2 tsp freshly ground pepper

Optional step: Trim lamb to expose 2" ends of bones (Frenching); protect exposed bones with a double thick layer of foil.

Combine ingredients; rub both racks of lamb with the mixture. (May be prepared to this point up to 4 hours ahead; cover and refrigerate. Return lamb to room temperature before roasting.)

Meanwhile, start a fire in the center of the oven floor. Keep oven fired for 2 hours. After flames subside, move embers against the oven walls. Place item to be roasted in center of oven; close door. Starting temperature for roasting should be 450F.

Place lamb, meaty side up, on a "V" rack positioned over a baking sheet to catch the drippings. Insert temperature probe in thickest part of meat. Roast in 450-500F oven (door closed, embers against walls) for 15-20 minutes, or until internal temperature registers 125F (medium rare). Remove from oven, tent with foil and let rest for 5 minutes before carving.

NOTE: Serve with white beans as shown, or with potatoes and haricots verts.
• *See DVD part 2/Section 10 for more on Roasting Lamb*

SUNDAY POT ROAST

What could be better on a lazy Sunday afternoon, than the smell of this roast coming from your woodfired oven?

Serves 6-8

1 4 lb. sirloin *or* rump roast
salt & pepper to taste

MARINADE
3 C red wine
1⁄4 C wine vinegar
1 C beef stock
1⁄2 C sliced onion
1⁄4 C sliced carrots
1 clove garlic, minced
1 T dried thyme
1 sprig parsley
1 bay leaf
1 T tomato paste

FOR BRAISING
4 T olive oil
reserved marinade

1 C sliced yellow onion
2 C sliced potatoes (or very small whole red, new potatoes)
2 C sliced carrots
1⁄2 C chopped parsley (for garnish)

Place roast in glass or enamel bowl, or in a large plastic food storage bag. Combine marinade ingredients; pour over roast. Marinate overnight in refrigerator.

Remove beef from marinade; pat dry with paper towels. Strain and reserve marinade liquid.

Meanwhile, start a fire in the center of the oven floor. Keep oven fired for 2-3 hours. After flames subside, move embers against the oven walls. Place item to be roasted in center of oven; close door. Starting temperature for roasting should be 450-500F.

Heat oil in Dutch oven (either stovetop or in the hot oven). Brown beef on all sides. Pour one cup marinade over roast and cover with lid. Place in 450 - 500F oven (no flame, embers against walls). After about 45 minutes, add vegetables around roast and add another cup of reserved marinade. Replace lid and close door of oven; continue cooking for approximately 45 minutes more, until meat is tender and vegetables are done.

Remove roast from oven and cover with foil; let rest for 20 minutes. Slice roast and arrange on serving platter; surround with vegetables. Pour pan juices over all, season with salt and freshly ground black pepper to taste. Garnish with chopped parsley.
• *See DVD part 2/Section 10 for more on Roasting*

PRIME RIB ROAST

The king of roasts, prepared simply to let the true flavors shine through. Your guests will rave about this recipe.

Serves 6–8

1 5-6 lb. prime rib roast of beef, trimmed of excess fat
3 T butter
3 cloves garlic, chopped
1 tsp chopped rosemary
1 T chopped fresh thyme
½ tsp salt
½ tsp freshly ground pepper
2 T olive oil

Make a paste using butter, garlic and herbs. Cut six ¾" slits in meaty part of roast, and pack each slit with herb mixture. Rub roast with olive oil, season with salt and pepper, and wrap in foil. Refrigerate 4 hours or overnight.

Meanwhile, start a fire in the center of the oven floor. Keep oven fired for 2 hours. After flames subside, move embers against the oven walls. Place item to be roasted in center of oven; close door. Starting temperature for roasting should be 500F.

Allow meat to return to room temperature before roasting (about 1½ hours). Place roast, bone side down, on rack in shallow baking dish and tent roast with double thickness of foil for first 30 minutes of cooking. Bake at 500F (no flame, door closed, embers against walls) until internal temperature registers 120 - 125F for medium rare (140F for medium) on meat thermometer, approximately 90 minutes altogether. Remove from oven, tent with foil and let rest 10 minutes before carving.

• *See DVD part 2/Section 10 for more on Roasting*

SIDES etc.

ARTICHOKE HEARTS GRATINEE

*A really nice first course, this also makes a great accompaniment
to virtually any meat dish*

Serves 6

6 large artichoke hearts, precooked
3 T olive oil
1 onion, chopped
1 bell pepper, roasted, peeled and chopped
in ¼" dice
2 tomatoes, peeled* and chopped in ¼" dice
1 C zucchini, chopped in ¼" dice
1 C eggplant, chopped in ¼" dice
1 clove garlic, finely chopped
½ C chicken broth
bouquet garni (2 sprigs thyme, 1 bay leaf, 2
sprigs parsley, tied in piece of cheesecloth)
salt and freshly ground pepper
6 T bread crumbs
6 T grated gruyere cheese

Start a fire in the center of the oven floor.
Keep oven fired for 11/2-2 hours. After
flames subside, move embers against the
oven walls. Place item to be roasted
in center of oven; close door. Starting
temperature for roasting should be 400-
500F.

Heat 1 tablespoon of olive oil in skillet.
Cook onions and bell peppers until onions
are translucent and peppers are soft. Add tomatoes and cook about 2 minutes.

In separate skillet, heat 1 tablespoon of oil and
cook zucchini until softened. Add to tomatoes
and onions. In remaining tablespoon of oil,
cook eggplant until softened and add to other
vegetables. Add garlic, chicken broth and bouquet garni, season with salt and pepper, and simmer for 10 minutes, or until liquid is absorbed.
Discard bouquet garni.

Brush a 7" x 7" square, or 9" round, baking dish
with melted butter. Arrange artichoke hearts
in dish and fill each with some of the vegetable
mixture. Top each with breadcrumbs, then
cheese.

Bake in 400-500F oven (door closed, embers
against walls) until nicely browned.

**To peel tomatoes: Drop tomatoes in boiling water
for 30 seconds, just until skins start to split; pull
them out and immerse in cold water to stop cooking.
Skins should come right off.*
• *See DVD part 2/Section 10 for more on Roasting*

GRILLED RADICCHIO

Although radicchio is fairly bitter when raw, it takes on a surprisingly mellow flavor when grilled. Try this unusual and delightful side dish with grilled chicken.

Serves 8

3 T olive oil
3 T balsamic vinegar
1 tsp Dijon mustard
4 large heads radicchio, quartered

Start a fire in the center of the oven. Keep fire burning for 45 minutes to 1 hour. Make sure you have enough embers to grill radicchio.

Spread embers on the floor of oven slightly larger than the size of the grill. Burning logs can be pushed to one side. Slide grill over embers and preheat for 5 minutes. Pull grill out and, using a clean rag or paper towel, lubricate grate with olive oil. Place items to be grilled on grate and slide back over embers.

Whisk oil, vinegar and mustard. until emulified. Trim away some of the thick white core from each radicchio quarter, leaving just enough core intact to hold leaves together while grilling.

Brush radicchio with balsamic mixture and grill for 1 minute on each side, or until nicely wilted.

NOTE: for a rich and smooth variation on this dish, try melting a thin slice of smoked mozzarella on top of each quartered radicchio piece just before the grilling is finished.

• See DVD part 1/Section 4 for more on Grilling

ROASTED NEW POTATOES

A versatile and hearty side dish, bursting with the bold flavors of Provence – or make a whole meal of these potatoes, with a salad on the side! Yes, they're that good.

Serves 4-6

2 lbs. red new potatoes, about 1½" in diameter, or cut to size
2 T olive oil
2 T chopped fresh rosemary

DRESSING
3 T olive oil
2 T red wine vinegar
1 T fresh lemon juice
1 T crushed garlic (2-3 cloves)
salt and pepper to taste
1 T chopped parsley
1 T chopped scallions
1 T chopped fresh basil
¼ C imported black olives

Start a fire in the center of the oven floor. After half an hour of firing, move the burning wood to the center left or center right. Keep the fire burning until the temperature gauge registers at least 550F.

Using the ash stick, move the embers to the side of the oven which will be most visible from the outside. You may start roasting when the temperature reaches 600F.

In large bowl, toss potatoes with olive oil and rosemary. Transfer to a large skillet or shallow roasting pan.

Roast in 600F oven (door off, and "pizza fire" burning) for about 15 minutes, or until fork tender. Stir potatoes once or twice during cooking to prevent sticking.

While potatoes are roasting, prepare dressing by whisking together all ingredients except olives.

When potatoes are done, toss with dressing and olives; serve warm or at room temperature.
• *See DVD part 1/Section 12 for more on Roasted New Potatoes*

ONION SOUP

This is as French as it gets! On a cool evening,
this soup and a green salad make a perfect meal.

Serves 6

3 large onions, thinly sliced
1 T butter
1 T vegetable oil
2 T flour
6 C chicken stock
1/2 C white wine
2 T cognac (optional)
salt and pepper to taste
6 slices country bread, cut just to fit inside
serving bowls
3 C grated gruyere or Swiss cheese

Start a fire in the center of the oven floor.
Keep oven fired for 11/2-2 hours. After
flames subside, move embers against
the oven walls. Place items in center of
oven; close door. Cooking temperature
should be 500F.

In large saucepan over low heat, cook onions
in butter and oil until translucent and golden,
stirring occasionally. Sprinkle flour over onions
and stir for 2 - 3 minutes. Add stock, wine and
cognac, if desired. Bring to a boil, then reduce
heat and simmer for 15 minutes. Adjust seasoning with salt and pepper.

Divide soup evenly among 6 ovenproof bowls.
Sprinkle 1/4 cup of cheese over each dish and
top with a slice of bread. Distribute remaining
cheese evenly over each dish.

Bake in 500F oven (door closed, embers against
walls) for 10 minutes, or until cheese is golden.
• *See DVD part 2/Section 10 for more on Roasting*

ZUCCHINI au GRATIN

*Another great first course, this versatile recipe pairs equally well
with chicken or fish as a side dish.*

Serves 4

4 medium zucchini squash, 2" x 7"
3 T olive oil
1 C diced onions
2 cloves garlic, chopped fine
4 oz. cooked ham, diced
2 T chopped parsley
1/2 tsp dried thyme
salt and pepper
1 C bread crumbs
1 C shredded mozzarella cheese

Start a fire in the center of the oven floor.
Keep oven fired for 11/2-2 hours. After
flames subside, move embers against
the oven walls. Place item to be roasted
in center of oven; close door. Starting
temperature for roasting should be 400-
500F.

Slice each zucchini in half lengthwise. Using
a melon baller or small spoon, carefully scoop
out pulp, leaving 1/4" wall and shell intact. Chop
pulp and set aside.

Place zucchini 'boats' in ovenproof dish. Pat
cavities dry, then brush inside and out with 1 T
of olive oil.

In skillet, heat remaining 2 T of olive oil. Cook
onions until translucent; add garlic and cook for
1 minute more. Add reserved zucchini pulp,
ham, parsley and thyme. Season to taste with
salt and pepper. Cook for 5 minutes.

Fill zucchini 'boats' with vegetable mixture. Top
with bread crumbs and cheese.

Bake in 400-500F oven (door closed, embers
against wall) for about 10 minutes, until zuc-
chinis are tender and cheese is browned.

• See DVD part 2/Section 10 for more on Roasting

SCALLOPED POTATOES au GRATIN

The one and only, the original, rich and creamy scalloped potatoes.
Why mess with potato perfection?

Serves 4-6

4 medium potatoes
¼ C butter
2 cloves garlic, finely chopped
¾ C milk or cream
½ tsp salt
½ tsp freshly ground pepper
½ tsp dried thyme
¼ C bread crumbs
½ C grated gruyere cheese

Start a fire in the center of the oven floor. Keep oven fired for 11/2-2 hours. After flames subside, move embers against the oven walls. Place item to be baked in center of oven; close door. Starting temperature for baking should be 500F.

Peel and thinly slice potatoes; keep them in cold salted water to avoid discoloration.

Heat butter in small saucepan. Add garlic and cook for 1 minute.

Brush a 7" x 7" square, or 9" round, baking dish with melted butter. Drain potatoes and pat dry with paper towels. Overlapping each slice slightly, arrange one layer in baking dish; brush with butter and top with half the salt, pepper and thyme; repeat with second layer. Combine milk together with any remaining butter and pour evenly over top of potatoes. Sprinkle with bread crumbs and cheese.

Cover dish with foil and bake in 500F oven (door closed, embers against wall) for 30 minutes. Remove foil and continue baking until potatoes are tender, about 1 hour more.

• *See DVD part 2/Section 10 for more on Roasting*

RATATOUILLE

Traditionally, ratatouille is made with all the vegetables cooked separately, then layered in a casserole and baked briefly in the oven. It makes for a beautiful presentation and separation of flavors, but frankly, this recipe is easier and just as tasty.

Serves 6-8

1 lb. eggplant, peeled and cut into 1" x ¼" pieces
2 lbs. zucchini, peeled and cut into 1" x ¼" pieces
1 large green bell pepper, cut into ¾" dice
1 large red bell pepper, cut into ¾" dice
1 large onion, diced
2 cloves garlic, finely chopped
½ lb. tomatoes, peeled*, seeded and chopped
½ tsp salt
½ tsp freshly ground black pepper
½ tsp dried thyme, or 1 T fresh
1 bay leaf
3 T olive oil
½ C chicken broth

1 T chopped parsley
1 T chopped fresh basil

Start a fire in the center of the oven floor. Keep oven fired for 2 hours. After flames subside, move embers against the oven walls. Place item to be baked in center of oven; close door. Starting temperature for baking should be 400-500F.

In large metal or ovenproof enamel, ceramic or clay pot* with cover, place all ingredients (except parsley and basil) and toss well.

*If using clay pot as shown, soak pot and lid in water for 1/2 hour prior to using, then temper the filled pot by heating slowly near the oven door before placing inside the oven.

Cover pot and place in 400-500F oven (no fire, door closed).

After about 30 minutes, gently mix vegetables. If necessary, add more chicken broth. There should be ½" of liquid in bottom of pot. Cook 30 minutes more, or until vegetables are 'al dente'. If there seems to be an excessive amount of liquid, cook uncovered for 10 more minutes. Adjust seasoning as needed.

Add parsley and basil; mix gently. Let rest for 20 minutes. May be served hot or cold.

NOTE: You may substitute butternut squash as shown, in place of zucchini for firmer texture, brighter color and a more assertively sweet-roasted flavor.

*To peel tomatoes: Drop tomatoes in boiling water for 30 seconds, just until skins start to split; pull them out and immerse in cold water to stop cooking. Skins should come right off.
• *See DVD part 2/Section 10 for more on Roasting*

DESSERTS

CLAFOUTIS

Traditional recipes leave the pits in the cherries during baking, but it's so much easier to eat with the pits removed. Clafoutis is wonderful during peak cherry season – or make this homey dessert anytime of year with red seedless grapes.

Serves 6-8

1 pie crust, chilled (recipe follows)
¼ C sugar
2 T cornstarch
½ tsp salt
2 eggs
1 tsp vanilla extract
2 C milk
2 T melted butter
2 C pitted fresh cherries *or* seedless red grapes
powdered sugar for dusting

Place chilled dough between 2 sheets of wax paper and roll out to 1/8" thickness, and 1" in diameter larger than 10" glass or ceramic tart pan. Drape dough over rolling pin and transfer to tart pan. Gently press dough into place, doubling over edge to form rim. Crimp edge using fingers or a small spoon. With a fork, prick dough all over to prevent crust from bubbling. Refrigerate dough for 30 minutes or more.

Meanwhile, start a fire in the center of the oven floor. Keep oven fired for 11/2-2 hours. After flames subside, move embers against the oven walls. Place item to be baked in center of oven; close door. Starting temperature for baking should be 450F.

While dough is chilling, prepare custard filling: in a bowl, combine sugar, cornstarch and salt. Mix in eggs and vanilla. Gradually incorporate milk and melted butter.

Line chilled tart shell with foil and fill with pie weights, dried beans or rice. Place weighted tart shell in 450F oven (door closed) and bake "blind" for about 5 minutes. Remove foil and weights, and bake another 5 minutes. Crust should be dry, but not colored. Remove from oven.

Evenly layer fruit in pie shell. Pour batter over fruit and return to oven (door closed). After 30 - 40 minutes, crust should be nicely browned and knife inserted in center should come out clean; dessert will fall slightly as it cools. Dust with powdered sugar before serving.

PIE CRUST
2 C all-purpose flour
½ tsp salt
1 T sugar
1 stick cold butter, cut in 1/2" pieces
1 egg
3 T water

In a food processor, pulse dry ingredients together. Add chilled butter and pulse until butter is pea-sized. Add egg and water, and pulse just until combined. The dough should not form a ball while mixing.

Shape dough into a ball by hand. Lightly flour dough and place between two pieces of plastic wrap. With rolling pin, flatten dough to a 6" circle, using additional flour as necessary to prevent sticking. Refrigerate dough for 20-30 minutes before using.

• *See DVD part 2/Section 9 for more on Baking*

GENOISE CAKE

*Whip up one of these after baking bread – the oven temperature
will be about 400-425F, just right for this delicate cake.*

Serves 10–12

butter
flour
6 large eggs
1 C sugar
1 T vanilla extract
1 C unbleached all-purpose flour
1⁄2 C melted unsalted butter, cooled

Start a fire in the center of the oven floor.
Keep it burning for 11⁄2 - 2 hours, maintaining a temperature of 450 - 500F. Let fire
burn out. Push embers to one side. Using a
long-handled peel or ashpan, shovel embers
into large metal pot containing 2" of water.
Carefully cover (very hot) pot with lid and
remove to a fireproof surface to cool. Brush
remaining ashes to one corner of oven floor.
Close oven door for 20 - 30 min. Remove
door carefully – it will be very hot! Place
item to be baked in center of oven; close
door. Starting temperature for baking
should be 400-425F.

Cut two pieces of wax paper into 9-inch
rounds. Butter and flour each round and fit
in bottom of two 9-inch cake pans. Butter
and flour inside walls of cake pans; set aside.

In mixer bowl, combine eggs, sugar and vanilla;
mix well. Set bowl over a saucepan containing 1" of hot water (bottom of bowl should not
touch water). Place saucepan/bowl over low
heat; stir egg mixture until warm. Return bowl
to mixer and beat eggs for about 10 minutes,
until tripled in volume. Sprinkle with flour and
fold gently by hand. Add cooled butter and fold
again until flour and butter are well incorporated. Do not overmix.

Divide batter between cake pans. Bake in 400-
425F oven (no embers, door closed) for about
15 - 20 minutes, or until cakes are golden and a
wood skewer inserted in center comes out clean.

Let cakes cool for 5 minutes, then invert cakes
on rack to cool thoroughly.

NOTE: Each cake may be sliced in half
horizontally if desired and layered with lightly
sweetened whipped cream.

• *See DVD part 2/Section 11 for more on Baking*

FLOURLESS CHOCOLATE SOUFFLÉ

Soufflés get a bad rap here in America, but there's really no reason to be afraid of preparing them. Try these, and you'll see what I mean!

Serves 8

butter
sugar

2 T hot water + 2 T butter
¾ C semisweet chocolate chips, or 5 oz chopped semisweet chocolate
4 egg yolks
1 tsp Grand Marnier
1 C sugar
4 egg whites
½ tsp cream of tartar

Start a fire in the center of the oven floor. After flames subside, move embers against the oven walls. Place item to be baked in center of oven; close door. Starting temperature for baking should be 450F.

Butter insides of eight 8-ounce ramekins; dust with sugar.

In heavy-bottomed saucepan, melt butter in hot water. Add chocolate and stir over low heat until completely melted. Remove from heat.

Beat egg yolks in mixer at medium speed for 1 minute. Add ¾ cup of the sugar, 1 tablespoon at a time, mixing 30 seconds after each addition until light and fluffy. Add chocolate mixture and Grand Marnier, and mix for 30 seconds, scraping side of bowl with spatula.

In a clean mixing bowl, beat egg whites with cream of tartar until soft peaks form. Add remaining sugar, 1 tablespoon at a time, beating 30 seconds after each addition, until stiff, glossy peaks form when beater is lifted.

Fold ¼ of the egg whites into the chocolate; gently fold the rest of the egg whites into the chocolate until well incorporated. Fill ramekins two-thirds full. Smooth and wipe inside edges of ramekins with your finger to insure even rising (batter will catch on any rough surfaces, which inhibits rising).

Bake in 450F oven (door closed) for about 15 minutes, or until soufflé forms a nice tall crown and crust (center should be soft). Serve immediately, with whipped cream if desired.

• See DVD part 2/Section 9 for more on Baking

MIXED BERRY CROUSTADE

This simple, rustic dessert makes a memorable ending to any meal. Substitute other seasonal berries, or use frozen berries any time of year.

Serves 8

1⁄2 C sugar
3 T cornstarch
2 C blueberries
2 C strawberries
1 T lemon juice

1 pie crust, chilled (recipe follows)
melted butter
raw sugar

In a large bowl, mix sugar and cornstarch. Add berries and lemon juice; combine well.

In a saucepan, bring 2/3 of the mixture to a slow boil, stirring constantly, for 2 minutes. Remove from heat and let cool. Fold in the remaining berry mixture. (May be done up to one day ahead and refrigerated. Allow berries to return to room temperature before proceeding.)

Roll out pie crust to 14" circle, using a plate as a guide. Transfer crust to 11" or 12" cardboard cake disk, or well-floured 10" plate, for support. Brush crust with melted butter, and then pour fruit mixture in center of crust. Spread filling evenly, allowing an approximate 3" edge.

Evenly fold exposed dough inward over the filling, creating a series of rustic flaps all the way around. Brush the top of the dough flaps with melted butter and sprinkle liberally with raw sugar. Transfer assembled pie (still on support plate or cardboard) to refrigerator for 1 - 4 hours.

Meanwhile, start a fire in the center of the oven floor. After flames subside, move embers against the oven walls. Place item to be baked in center of oven; close door. Starting temperature for baking should be 500F.

Preheat a cast iron flat plate or aluminum pizza tray in 500F oven (embers against the walls or no embers; door closed). To bake, carefully slide chilled pie from its support plate directly onto preheated metal tray in 500F oven for 15 - 20 minutes (door closed), or until crust is nice and brown and fruit is bubbly. Serve warm or at room temperature, with a dollop of whipped cream if desired.

PIE CRUST
2 C all-purpose flour
1⁄2 tsp salt
1 T sugar
1 stick cold butter, cut in 1/2" pieces
1 egg
3 T water

In a food processor, pulse dry ingredients together. Add chilled butter and pulse until butter is pea-sized. Add egg and water, and pulse just until combined. The dough should not form a ball while mixing.

Shape dough into a ball by hand. Lightly flour dough and place between two pieces of plastic wrap. With rolling pin, flatten dough to a 6" circle, using additional flour as necessary to prevent sticking. Refrigerate dough for 20-30 minutes before using.

• *See DVD part 2/Section 9 for more on Baking*

TARTE aux AMANDES ALMOND TART

We had 15 almond trees on our farm. My mother used bitter almonds in place of almond extract – and a mortar and pestle instead of a food processor. In those days, this tart was made with pie crust; puff pastry makes it lighter and more refined.

Serves 8

1 C whole almonds
1 C sugar
2 eggs
¼ C (or 2 oz.) butter, room temperature
1 tsp almond extract
2 sheets puff pastry, 8 oz. each
egg yolk + 2 T water, for brushing

Start a fire in the center of the oven floor. Keep it burning for 1½ - 2 hours, maintaining a temperature of 450 - 500F. Let fire burn out. Push embers to one side. Using a long-handled peel or ashpan, shovel embers into large metal pot containing 2" of water. Carefully cover (very hot) pot with lid and remove to a fireproof surface to cool. Brush remaining ashes to one corner of oven floor. Close oven door for 20 - 30 min. Remove door carefully – it will be very hot! Place item to be baked in center of oven; close door. Starting temperature for baking should be 450F.

In a food processor fitted with a metal blade, grind almonds and sugar until fine. Add eggs, butter and almond extract. Mix 5 seconds; scrape sides of bowl and mix 3 seconds more. Refrigerate.

Roll out each sheet of puff pastry to a 10" square. With the aid of a plate, cut a 9" circle from each sheet of pastry (save dough corners for decorating tart).

Place one pastry circle on a floured wood disk or round piece of cardboard. Spread almond mixture evenly on the pastry, leaving a 1" border. Brush border with water and place second pastry circle on top. Crimp edges with a fork to seal completely. Refrigerate at least 30 minutes or up to 4 hours.

Beat egg yolk together with 2 T water; brush top of tart with egg mixture before baking. If desired, mold or cut saved pastry dough scraps into shapes and decorate top of tart. Prick top of tart to let steam escape.

To bake, place a flat, cast iron plate in a 450F oven (no embers) to preheat for 5 minutes. Slide tart onto preheated cast iron plate and return to oven (door closed). When tart has turned a dark golden color (about 15-20 minutes), remove from oven. Let cool for 10-15 minutes. Cut into wedges and serve.

• See DVD part 2/Section 9 for more on Baking

PEAR-CRANBERRY STRUDEL

Apples can be substituted instead of the pears, if you like. When working with phyllo dough, keep any sheets not immediately in use covered with plastic wrap or a barely moist dish towel. Reseal and store any unused phyllo as soon as possible.

Makes 2 strudels

3 - 4 Bosc or other firm pears, peeled, cored and cut in 1/2" dice, (enough to make 3 C)
1 T lemon juice
1⁄2 C finely chopped walnuts
1⁄2 C dried cranberries
1⁄2 tsp cinnamon
1⁄2 C sugar
1 tsp vanilla
1 T cornstarch
1⁄2 C butter
4 sheets phyllo dough

Start a fire in the center of the oven floor. Keep it burning for 11⁄2 - 2 hours, maintaining a temperature of 450 - 500F. Let fire burn out. Push embers to one side. Using a long-handled peel or ashpan, shovel embers into large metal pot containing 2" of water. Carefully cover (very hot) pot with lid and remove to a fireproof surface to cool. Brush remaining ashes to one corner of oven floor. Close oven door for 20 - 30 min. Remove door carefully – it will be very hot! Place item to be baked in center of oven; close door. Starting temperature for baking should be 450F.

Toss diced pears with lemon juice, walnuts, cranberries, cinnamon, sugar, vanilla and cornstarch.

In 12" skillet, melt 1⁄4 cup of the butter. Pour pear mixture in skillet and cook over medium heat, stirring constantly, until fruit is just softened. Let cool.

Melt remaining 1⁄4 cup butter. Using 2 sheets of wax paper, overlap as necessary to make an 18" X 24" rectangle. Place 1 sheet of phyllo on wax paper and brush lightly with melted butter; repeat with second sheet of phyllo, layering it on top of the first sheet. Place half of fruit mixture lengthwise along lower third of phyllo, leaving 1" on each end (see diagram below). Fold 1" ends over filling and, using wax paper to help, gently roll long side of dough over filling, and once again, jellyroll style, to form a 16" long strudel. Remove wax paper. Place strudel on buttered baking sheet and brush top with melted butter. Repeat with remaining dough and filling to form a second strudel.

Cut each strudel into thirds, which allows it to bake more evenly and be served more easily. Bake in a 450F oven (door closed) for about 45 minutes, or until golden and bubbly. Let cool 10 minutes before slicing and serving.

• *See DVD part 2/Section 11 for more on Baking*

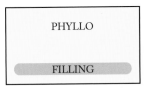

CLASSIC BREAD PUDDING

What better way to use up stale bread? Any good white bread will do, but brioche or challah will take your bread pudding over the top.

Serves 8

7 C day-old bread, cut in 1" cubes (French bread, plain focaccia, shepherd's bread or brioche)
1/2 C butter, melted
6 eggs
1/2 C sugar
4 C milk
1 T vanilla extract
1/2 tsp almond extract
1 tsp cinnamon

Arrange bread cubes on a baking sheet in a single layer. Dry in 400F oven for 15 minutes, stirring 2 or 3 times to prevent over-browning. (May be done 2 or 3 days ahead. Store dried bread cubes in zip-lock bag.)

Start a fire in the center of the oven floor. Keep oven fired for 11/2-2 hours. After flames subside, move embers against the oven walls. Place item to be baked in center of oven; close door. Starting temperature for baking should be 400-500F.

In large bowl, combine bread with melted butter; turn into 13 x 9" baking dish.

In another bowl, mix eggs, sugar, milk, extracts and cinnamon. Pour over bread cubes.

Bake in 400-500F oven (door closed, embers against walls) for 30 minutes, or until knife inserted in middle comes out clean. Do not overbake. (If top browns too quickly, cover with aluminum foil.)

Serve warm or at room temperature topped with Crème Anglaise (see recipe, below), if desired.

CRÈME ANGLAISE
1 C milk
3 egg yolks
1/3 C sugar
1/2 tsp vanilla extract

Heat milk to just before boiling point; meanwhile combine egg yolks, sugar and vanilla in a medium bowl. Beat egg mixture with a wire whisk until it becomes light and fluffy. Add the scalded milk very slowly to the egg mixture*, beating the mixture vigorously the whole time.

When combined, place mixture into a double boiler (or a metal bowl set over a pot of simmering water) over low heat, and continue stirring with a wooden spoon until the mixture coats the back of the spoon. Can be served warm or cold.

*By adding the hot milk very slowly to the eggs and beating continuously, you'll keep the egg mixture cool enough to prevent a bowl of milky scrambled eggs instead of silky crème.
• See DVD part 2/Section 9 for more on Baking

APRICOT CRUMBLE

Fresh peaches can be substituted for the apricots; or for a tangy, tropical alternative, substitute sliced, unpeeled guavas (seeds removed), when in season. Increase sugar for guavas to 3/4 cup.

Serves 8

1 recipe Crumble Crust (recipe follows)

4 C sliced apricots
1⁄2 C sugar
1⁄4 C all purpose flour

Start a fire in the center of the oven floor. Keep oven fired for 11/2-2 hours. After flames subside, move embers against the oven walls. Place item to be baked in center of oven; close door. Starting temperature for baking should be 450F.

In a large bowl, combine fruit, flour and sugar. Mix well.

Divide crumble crust into two portions. Cover bottom of 10" ovenproof pie pan (glass, ceramic or metal) with half the crust mixture. Arrange fruit over dough. Top with remaining crust mixture.

Bake in 450F oven (door closed) for approximately 45 minutes, or until filling is bubbling and crust is nicely browned.

CRUMBLE CRUST
1 C flour
1⁄2 C sugar
1⁄2 C cold butter, cut into 1⁄2" pieces
1 C finely chopped pecans or walnuts

In a large bowl, combine flour and sugar. Using a pastry cutter or two knives, cut butter into flour mixture until it resembles coarse meal. Add the chopped nuts and mix with a spoon.

• See DVD part 2/Section 9 for more on Baking

APPLE PIE "PIZZA"

Not a true dessert pizza, this is actually a single crust pie that's baked flat like a pizza – but it tastes more like a rustic tart.

Serves 8

PIE CRUST
2 C unbleached all-purpose flour
½ tsp salt
2 T sugar
1 stick cold butter, cut into ½" pieces
2 T ice water
1 egg, refrigerated

In the bowl of a food processor fitted with metal blade, place flour, salt, sugar and butter. Pulse 5 or 6 times until the mixture resembles small peas. (Alternatively, you may do this by hand using two knives to achieve the same result.) Add water and egg, and pulse just until mixture holds together.

Turn dough out onto well-floured surface and knead gently; form into a ball. Flatten into a ¾" thick disk, wrap in plastic and refrigerate for at least ½ hour, or overnight.

Remove dough from refrigerator and let rest for 5 minutes. Roll dough into a 15" circle. Using a pie plate or dish as a guide, trim dough into an even 14" circle. Working quickly, fold ½" edge over and crimp, using thumb and forefinger. Prick dough with a fork and place on floured board; cover with plastic wrap and freeze for at least ½ hour, or overnight. (This recipe may be used for any pie crust.)

APPLE TOPPING
2 apples (Granny Smith, Red Delicious or Pippin)
juice of ½ lemon
½ C apricot jelly
2 tsp Grand Marnier or Cointreau

Peel, core and slice apples lengthwise into 1/8" slices. Place in non-reactive bowl and drizzle with lemon juice; toss well to coat.

Mix apricot jelly with Grand Marnier. Brush frozen pastry shell with half of apricot mixture. Arrange apple slices, overlapping, in single layer. Brush fruit with remaining apricot mixture. Refrigerate pie for 15 minutes or up to 2 hours before baking.

Meanwhile, start a fire in the center of the oven floor. Keep oven fired for 1 1/2-2 hours. After flames subside, move embers against the oven walls. Starting temperature for baking should be 450F.

Mop floor of oven with a damp towel to cool slightly, otherwise the high fat content of the pie crust will cause the bottom to brown too quickly. This crust is fragile and must be handled gently. Bake in 450F oven (door closed) for approximately 10-15 minutes, or until filling is bubbling and crust is nicely browned.

• See DVD part 2/Section 9 for more on Baking

CALVADOS APPLE CAKE

You may also make this versatile cake using fresh apricots instead of apples, if you prefer; just omit the cinnamon and use Grand Marnier instead of the Calvados.

Serves 10-12

6 small tart apples
juice of ½ lemon
3 T sugar
1 T cinnamon
½ C butter
¾ C sugar
2 eggs, separated
½ lemon, juiced and zested
1 tsp baking powder
1½ C all purpose flour
¾ C milk
1 tsp vanilla
1 T Calvados
1 T butter
3 T powdered sugar

Start a fire in the center of the oven floor. Keep it burning for 1½ - 2 hours, maintaining a temperature of 450 - 500F. Let fire burn out. Push embers to one side. Using a long-handled peel or ashpan, shovel embers into large metal pot containing 2" of water. Carefully cover (very hot) pot with lid and remove to a fireproof surface to cool. Brush remaining ashes to one corner of oven floor. Close oven door for 20 - 30 min. Remove door carefully – it will be very hot! Place item to be baked in center of oven; close door. Starting temperature for baking should be 400F.

Peel, halve and core apples. Make 7 or 8 lengthwise slits (approx. ½" deep) on each half and toss with lemon juice, sugar and cinnamon. Set aside.

Cream butter and sugar together in a bowl until light and fluffy. Beat in egg yolks, one at a time (reserve whites). Beat in lemon juice and zest.

Sift baking powder and flour together in another bowl. In separate bowl, combine milk, vanilla and brandy. Add half of flour mixture to the creamed butter. Incorporate milk mixture, and finish with remaining flour mixture.

Beat reserved egg whites until stiff. Fold into batter.

Butter a 10" springform pan. Pour in batter. Top with apple halves. Brush apples with melted butter.

Bake in oven at 400F for 35 minutes; cake is done when wooden skewer inserted in middle comes out clean. Sprinkle with powdered sugar.

NOTE: the 400F baking temperature makes this a perfect dessert to whip up following a session of bread baking)
• *See DVD part 2/Section 11 for more on Baking*

BANANA PIZZA

Virtually any fruit or sweet topping can be baked onto a dessert pizza - let your imagination be your guide.

Makes one pizza

11" pizza (made from 8 oz. dessert pizza dough at room temperature - recipe follows on next page)
2 large bananas, ripe but not soft, sliced 1/8" thick
juice of 1/2 lemon
2 T brown sugar
4 T apricot jelly
5 T sour cream
Chocolate Sauce (recipe follows)
Grand Marnier Whipped Cream (recipe follows)

Start a fire in the center of the oven floor. After half an hour of firing, move the burning wood to the center left or center right. Keep the fire burning until the temperature gauge registers at least 550F. Using the ash stick, move the embers to the side of the oven which will be most visible from the outside. You may start baking pizza when the temperature reaches 600-700F.

Place bananas in small glass or plastic container, drizzle with lemon juice and sprinkle with brown sugar. Combine well and set aside.

Prick pizza shell all over with fork. Par-bake shell near door opening using a pizza fire (door off, flame to one side). This crust will brown very quickly. Remove from oven and allow to cool. (May be done the day before if desired.)

Spread par-baked shell with apricot jelly, leaving 1/2" border around edge. Layer sour cream, and then banana slices. Pour leftover banana liquid evenly over top.

Bake in 600 - 700F oven near door (fire on, door off) for 3 to 4 minutes, or until crust is light brown. Remove and allow to rest for several minutes. Using a spoon or squeeze bottle, drizzle chocolate sauce decoratively over pizza. Slice and top with whipped cream.

CHOCOLATE SAUCE
3 oz. semisweet chocolate
1/4 C whipping cream
1 tsp Grand Marnier

Melt chocolate in a small, heavy-bottomed saucepan on very low heat, or in top of double boiler (water should be at a simmer and not touching upper pot). In separate pot, heat cream. When chocolate is melted, add cream and Grand Marnier. Stir until sauce has glossy sheen to it. (Sauce can be refrigerated and re-warmed in a hot water bath when needed.)

GRAND MARNIER WHIPPED CREAM
1 C whipping cream
2 T confectioner's sugar
1 tsp vanilla extract
1 tsp Grand Marnier

Whip cream with sugar until soft peaks form when mixer is lifted. Add vanilla and Grand Marnier. Mix for 5 more seconds.

• See DVD part 2/Section 8 for more on Dessert Pizza

DESSERT PIZZA DOUGH

makes three 8 oz. pizza shells

1 C all purpose flour (unbleached)
2 C cake flour
2 T instant dry yeast
2 T cold butter, cut in 1/2" pieces
1¼ C refrigerated bottled water
½ tsp salt
4 T sugar

Dissolve sugar and salt in cold water.

Reserving ½ cup of all purpose flour, put first three ingredients in mixer bowl. Attach paddle to electric mixer and mix at low speed for 3 seconds. Drop butter pieces into flour mixture and mix at low speed for 5 seconds. Add water and mix at low speed. Replace paddle with hook attachment and mix for 1 minute at low speed; increase setting to 2nd speed and add remaining 1/2 cup flour. Mix until dough is smooth, approximately 3 minutes.

Remove dough from bowl and knead by hand for 1 minute. Divide into 3 equal portions (each portion will make an 11" dessert pizza) and place in plastic bags or plastic container. Refrigerate 4 hours or overnight. (May be refrigerated for 2 days or frozen for up to 4 weeks. If frozen, dough should be allowed to thaw overnight in the refrigerator.)

Bring dough to room temperature for 1 hour before baking.

• *See DVD part 2/Section 8 for more on Dessert Pizza*

QUICK RUSTIC FIG BREAD

This is one of those simple, no-fuss desserts that you can put together in a flash, and bake it while the oven is still warm from the main course.

Serves 4

4 large slices of country bread
¼ C melted butter
6-8 large fresh figs
¼ C sugar
2 T powdered sugar

Start a fire in the center of the oven floor. Keep oven firing for 45 minutes - 1 hour. After flames subside, move embers against the oven walls. Place item to be baked in center of oven; close door. Starting temperature for baking should be 450-500F.

Place bread slices in a shallow, ovenproof ceramic dish, or metal roasting pan. Brush with melted butter.

Slice figs in eighths. Toss with sugar.

Arrange figs evenly over bread slices and bake at 450-500F (door closed) for 8 to 10 minutes, or until bread is crusty and fruit is soft and caramelized. Dust with powdered sugar and serve immediately.

• *See DVD part 2/Section 9 for more on Baking*

TARTE TATIN

One of the most famous French desserts of all time, and with good reason!

Serves 10–12

1 C sugar
3 T water
8 large apples (Red Delicious or Granny Smith)
1 T cinnamon
juice of ½ lemon
3 T butter

1 pie crust (recipe follows on next page)
or puff pastry may be substituted instead

Icing (recipe follows)
or vanilla ice cream

Combine sugar with water and cook in a 10" ovenproof skillet over medium heat until mixture turns a clear amber color; let cool.

Peel and core apples; cut 7 of them into quarters, and halve one for the center of the skillet. In large bowl, toss apples with lemon juice and cinnamon.

Arrange apples neatly in skillet, rounded side down. Place halved apple, cut side up, in center of skillet. Fill the skillet with remaining apples. Dot with small pieces of butter.
Cover skillet with slightly smaller lid to allow for evaporation of excess liquid. Cook on stovetop for 45 minutes on low heat, until apples are soft to touch. Let cool.

Roll chilled dough out to a circle 2" larger than the skillet, approximately 1/8" thick. Drape dough over rolling pin to assist in centering it over skillet. Using a knife, trim away excess from edge of skillet, and tuck dough just inside pan, hugging apples. Cover pan with foil and refrigerate at least 2 hours or overnight.

Meanwhile, start a fire in the center of the oven floor. Keep oven fired for 1 1/2-2 hours. After flames subside, move embers against the oven walls. Place item to be baked in center of oven; close door. Starting temperature for baking should be 500F.

Bake at 500F (door closed) until crust is golden brown, about 20 - 30 minutes.

Shake skillet to loosen apples from bottom of pan. Invert carefully onto serving platter.

ICING
1 C whipping cream
2 T powdered sugar
1 tsp vanilla extract
1 T Grand Marnier (optional)

Beat all ingredients together. Fill a pastry bag (or food storage bag with corner cut off) and pipe icing over each portion in zigzag design.
or serve with vanilla ice cream.
• See DVD part 2/Section 9 for more on Apple Tarte Tatin

PIE CRUST DOUGH

The secret to the crust is to work quickly with the dough so the butter does not have time to melt; this is what makes the crust flaky.

makes 1 pie crust

2 C all-purpose flour
1⁄2 tsp salt
1 T sugar
1 stick cold butter, cut in 1/2" pieces
1 egg
3 T water

By hand:
In a stainless steel bowl, place dry ingredients and mix well. Cut butter pieces into flour mixture using two knives or a pastry cutter, until the consistency of coarse cornmeal is achieved. Beat egg with water, and add to dough mixture as needed. Dough should barely hold together.

or Using food processor:
Pulse dry ingredients together. Add chilled butter and pulse until butter is pea-sized. Add egg and water, and pulse just until combined. The dough should not form a ball while mixing.

Shape dough into a ball. Lightly flour dough and place between two pieces of plastic wrap. With rolling pin, flatten dough to a 6-inch circle, using additional flour as necessary to prevent sticking. Refrigerate dough for 20 to 30 minutes before using.

Jean–Paul and Maurice take a break.

RECIPE LIST

RECILE LIST cont'd

MEATS

SIDES, etc.

DESSERTS

EARTHSTONE WOODFIRE OVENS

6717 San Fernando Road
Glendale CA 91201
800.840.4915
earthstone@earthlink.net
www.earthstoneovens.com

BOOK PHOTOGRAPHY & DESIGN:

Outwater Productions   818.335.8466
Triffet Design Group   805.658.8646